Woun[ ]
Sti[ ]

MW00774126

The American Indian Movement,
the FBI, and Their Fight to Bury
the Sins of the Past

Wounded Knee 1973: Still Bleeding

The American Indian Movement, the FBI, and Their Fight to Bury the Sins of the Past

Stew Magnuson

Court Bridge Publishing
Arlington, Virginia

Magnuson, Stew, 1963–
Wounded Knee 1973: Still Bleeding, The American Indian
Movement, the FBI, and their fight to bury the sins of the past
Includes bibliographical references, photos, map, index.
ISBN 978-0985299613

Map designed by Alexandra Stoicof
Front cover designed by Dulca Cipri. Courtesy of Now & Then
Reader.
Book designed by Dedicated Book Services (www.netdbs.com)
All photos by Stew Magnuson

*To Madeleine and Bahman Homayoonfar,
the best in-laws a new Dad could ever have*

CONTENTS

ILLUSTRATIONS

A NOTE FROM THE AUTHOR

Wounded Knee 1973: Still Bleeding is the print edition of an eBook produced by the Now & Then Reader, Chicago, Illinois, edited by Ivan R. Dee, and released in February 2013.

It was originally envisioned as a 10,000 word piece of long-form journalism giving a blow-by-blow account of the Dakota Conference at Augustana College April 27–28, 2012, which examined the Wounded Knee Occupation. It was the realization that the history conference was itself historic, which inspired this book. Never before had so many key figures from both sides of the divisive incident been under the same roof at the same time. It would also turn out to be one of American Indian Movement leader Russell Means' final opportunities to defend AIM.

While it swelled to nearly 30,000 words, this book is not intended to be a comprehensive account of the conference, the occupation and its aftermath. Many key incidents and figures have been omitted in the name of brevity. *Wounded Knee 1973: Still Bleeding* is intended to give an overview of the occupation, the conference and some of the unresolved issues that are certain to be discussed leading up to the 40th anniversary of the siege in February 2013. For more details, please search out of the more extensive books mentioned as sources in the back of the book.

Every effort was made to include the main points made by the participants at the conference. However, a word-for-word transcription of every presentation would not be compelling reading. The author set out to be as fair as possible. Meanwhile, he makes no apology for his biases—including asides in the story—his opinions and conclusions.

TIMELINE

July 1968—American Indian Movement (AIM) founded in St. Paul, Minnesota.

March 8, 1972—AIM marches on Gordon, Nebraska, to protest death of Raymond Yellow Thunder.

November 1–9, 1972—AIM participates in occupation of Bureau of Indian Affairs headquarters, Washington, D.C.

February 6, 1973—Custer Courthouse Riot.

February 27, 1973—AIM and local Oglala Lakotas occupy Wounded Knee, S.D.

May 5, 1973—Wounded Knee Occupation ends.

October 17, 1973—Pedro Bissonette shot by BIA police on Pine Ridge Reservation.

January 8, 1974—Trial of AIM leaders Dennis Banks and Russell Means begins in St. Paul, Minnesota.

Sept. 16, 1974—Leadership trial ends in dismissal.

June 26, 1975—FBI agents Ron Williams and Jack Coler killed after shootout with AIM members in Oglala, S.D.

February 24, 1976—Anna Mae Aquash found dead near Wanblee, S.D.

April 18, 1977—Leonard Peltier convicted and sentenced to two life terms in prison for murder of FBI agents.

November 3, 1999—Russell Means in Denver, Colorado, accuses AIM leaders of conspiring to murder Aquash.

February 13, 2004—Arlo Looking Cloud convicted of murdering Aquash.

October 13, 2007—AIM leader Vernon Bellecourt dies in Minneapolis, Minnesota.

December 10, 2010—John Graham convicted of murdering Aquash.

April 27–28, 2012—Augustana College in Sioux Falls, S.D. holds conference examining Wounded Knee Occupation.

October 22, 2012—Russell Means dies in Porcupine, S.D.

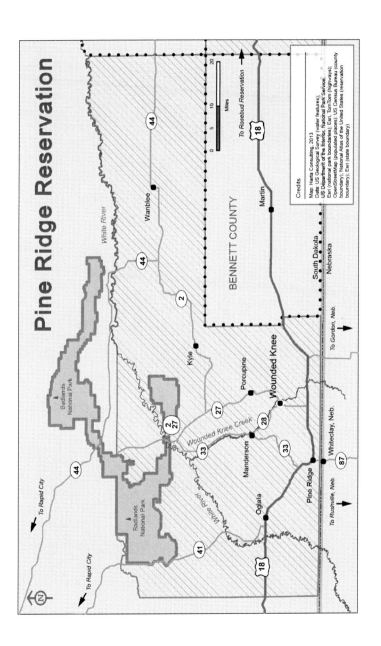

PRELUDES

It was an unseasonably warm winter day in 1890 on the Pine Ridge Indian Reservation in South Dakota when shells began to rain on the weary and half-starved band of Miniconjou Lakotas in the valley below.

A Paiute prophet to the west had spread a message of salvation from all the miseries the white man had perpetrated on the Indians. All they had to do was chant and dance, and the world would be reborn. The Ghost Dance religion swept over the prairie and spooked the white settlers, who believed their neighbors were engaged in a war dance. The United States cavalry had orders to intercept and disarm Chief Big Foot's people, who had broken away from their reservation to the north to join their Oglala Lakota cousins in the dance at the Pine Ridge Reservation. After finding the band near Wounded Knee Creek, the Bluecoats attempted to confiscate the Indians' firearms. The Lakotas didn't like that. A gun was fired—perhaps by accident—and then the slaughter began.

The Indian warriors fought in vain as shells and shrapnel from the Hotchkiss—a sort of half-cannon, half–machine gun—tore into their canvas tents. The Bluecoats emptied their repeating

1

rifles at anything that moved, sometimes killing one of their own by accident. Within minutes the engagement was decided, for no one could have withstood the withering fire for long. But the officer in charge failed to call for a cease-fire, so the massacre continued. Terrified women and children fled into the maze of gullies that led to Wounded Knee Creek as men and boys tried to help them escape. Bodies would later be found several miles from the camp.

When the bloodbath finally ended on that day, December 29, 1890, the Indian wounded were carted off and the dead left behind. They were eventually buried in a mass grave on a hilltop where the Hotchkiss had been mounted. The Lakotas called it a massacre. The army called it a battle and awarded Medals of Honor to twenty of its soldiers. The episode at Wounded Knee earned an infamy and symbolized the end of Native American resistance to the advancing American empire.

* * *

Eighty-two years and seventy days later, on the night of February 27, 1973, the resistance began again. A convoy of beat-up cars carrying dozens of angry young men sped into the same valley at Wounded Knee. A thin ribbon of blacktop now traversed the spot on the Pine Ridge Reservation where the ill-fated Lakotas had camped. A small trading post, a few residences, and a museum containing Indian artwork and artifacts stood beside the road. Next to the mass grave, a white chapel with a steeple overlooked the village close by.

The confused residents, most of them elderly whites or mixed-blood Indians, and one twelve-year-old girl, looked out their windows to see what was causing the commotion. When the men began shooting out the streetlights, they knew there was trouble. Members of the American Indian Movement (AIM) and local Lakotas had come to occupy Wounded Knee, to make a symbolic stand against injustice. They would hold out against the U.S. government for seventy-one days.

The angry Native American activists had occupied this symbolic site—where Chief Big Foot and members of his band had been slaughtered in 1890—to protest the "nontraditional" administration of Oglala Sioux Tribal Chairman Dick Wilson. But the occupation lasted more than two months and turned into something much bigger than a factional squabble on the reservation. The violence involved in the protest prompted attention to the wide range of injustices perpetrated on Native Americans. It produced headlines around the world, attracted scores of activists, and made celebrities of Dennis Banks and Russell Means, AIM leaders. By the time the occupiers left, the village had been destroyed. Two were dead, one went missing, and a U.S. marshal was left paralyzed. The sensational trial of Means and Banks on charges stemming from the incident lasted almost six months longer than the occupation itself. A dirty war between AIM, the FBI, and Oglalas loyal to Chairman Wilson continued for the remainder of the decade. Dozens died under mysterious circumstances in the years following the occupation, including one of Wilson's greatest rivals, Pedro Bissonette, who was killed in a shootout with police. Two FBI agents, Ron Williams and Jack Coler, were slaughtered in cold blood. Anna Mae Aquash, the highest-ranking woman among the protesters, was shot in the back of the head by one of her own.

APRIL 27, 2012

Almost forty years after the 1973 occupation at Wounded Knee, the Center for Western Studies at Augustana College in Sioux Falls, South Dakota, hosted its forty-fourth annual Dakota Conference. Following its usual pattern, the gathering at the private, Lutheran-run school was devoted to the history, culture, and literature of the upper Great Plains. It was a forum where professors and graduate students came to present the results of their latest research in half-hour sessions, where poets and novelists read passages from Western-themed books that sold hundreds and sometimes a few thousand copies.

But this year the conference would offer something different. The organizers had settled on a controversial theme: "Wounded Knee: Forty Years Later." It wasn't quite forty years since the American Indian Movement and its local allies had occupied the village on the Pine Ridge Reservation and sparked the first armed insurrection in the United States since the Civil War. But the takeover had begun in February 1973, and the conference was always held in April, so it was decided to mark the event in 2012.

Gusts swayed the trees outside the Center and augured a spring thundershower that would arrive that evening, just as Russell Means, gaunt from a recent bout with cancer of the esophagus, took the pulpit in the nearby Chapel of Reconciliation to deliver a speech titled "The Wounded Knee Occupation: Before, During, and After." The irony of the chapel's name should have been obvious for those conference participants who that afternoon had experienced sessions filled with angry words, insults, and murder accusations, where the words "lies" and "liar" had been heard a dozen times.

The conference that normally looked at history through an academic lens turned out to be historic itself. For this was the first time in memory that so many figures from the tumultuous 1973 occupation had gathered under the same roof. AIM co-founder Clyde Bellecourt had come from St. Paul, Minnesota, to join the discussions. Dennis Banks, another senior AIM leader, though not scheduled to participate, at the last minute had driven to Sioux Falls to defend his actions at the occupation. Joseph Trimbach, the FBI agent in charge during the first few weeks of the occupation, and his son John, both vehement AIM critics, led a panel discussion—"Revisiting Key Questions Concerning the 1973 Takeover and Occupation of Wounded Knee." With the Trimbachs were Cheryl Buswell, the widow of

Perry Ray Robinson, a black civil rights activist who had gone to Wounded Knee and disappeared there under mysterious circumstances. On a video feed was Denise Maloney, the daughter of Anna Mae Pictou-Aquash, a Canadian Mi'kmaq Indian, who had married in Wounded Knee but three years after the occupation was executed by two rank-and-file AIM members. Also present was Adrienne Fritze, who was twelve years old when dozens of men and women invaded the little hamlet and took her and her family hostage. Fritze, now fifty-one, had come to the conference in a spirit of reconciliation. All she wanted was an apology from those who had traumatized her and her family. She would not get it.

Means, Bellecourt, and Banks, all in their seventies, and Trimbach, by then in his eighties, came to fight for their good names. History had not been kind to any of them. Some of their supporters looked at them as heroes, but all four men had been painted as rogues by their opponents. Perhaps sensing that the conference would be their final opportunity to set the record straight, they journeyed to this small city on the banks of the Big Sioux River, to a college little known outside the state, where the winds were blowing up a storm.

Joining the discussions were others who came to defend these four elderly men. They included

David Price, a former FBI agent who was once the partner of Ron Williams, one of two FBI agents killed on Pine Ridge; Ward Churchill, a controversial left-wing academic and constant companion of Russell Means; former U.S. senator James Abourezk, a South Dakota lawmaker who during his one term as senator had gone to Wounded Knee to broker a deal between the protesters and the government; and Judge David Gienapp, a former prosecuting attorney who had tried and failed to convict Means and Banks for crimes allegedly committed during the siege. Kevin McKiernan, the last reporter to enter the village in 1973, delivered the first keynote remarks.

Thirty-nine years later, the anger stemming from the occupation and its turbulent aftermath had not cooled. Some observers believe that the Pine Ridge Reservation, one of the poorest places in the United States, still suffers from the trauma inflicted by the warring sides in the 1970s. The conference organizer at Augustana, Professor Harry Thompson, executive director of the Center for Western Studies, had spent a nearly sleepless night worrying about a rumored demonstration. Angry youths were said to be heading to the meeting. They never materialized, but Thompson asked campus police for increased security to keep an eye out for trouble.

THE CUSTER COURTHOUSE RIOT

The roots of the 1973 uprising lay in the indignities suffered by Clyde Bellecourt, Dennis Banks, and other Ojibwe Indians from Minnesota living in the so-called Indian slums of Minneapolis, where poverty and police brutality was rife. In 1968, deciding that it was time for a more assertive brand of Native American activism, they founded the American Indian Movement. Martin Luther King, Jr., was dead. His nonviolent, turn-the-other-cheek brand of social protest was evolving into something more aggressive. "Black Power" and "Chicano Power" were new slogans. If someone slapped your cheek, you slapped back. Like African Americans and Mexican Americans, Indians had been on the receiving end of more than their fair measure of injustice. AIM set out to put an end to it: "Red Power" had arrived. Native Americans, who had been kicked around for five hundred years, weren't going to be kicked around anymore. AIM chapters quickly spread to cities throughout the nation, where pockets of Indians had moved from their reservations to find jobs.

The movement's first foray outside urban areas came in March 1972, when AIM gathered on the Pine Ridge Reservation in South Dakota to demand justice for the death of Raymond Yellow Thunder, a Lakota ranch worker who had been abducted by four white men in the town of Gordon, Nebraska, beaten, and shoved half-naked into the local American Legion hall while a dance was in progress. He was found dead eight days later in the front of an old truck in a used-car lot. AIM leaders, who until then were seen as big-city intellectuals, had been looking for ways to win support on reservations. The case of Raymond Yellow Thunder was their opportunity. AIM gathered supporters from reservations throughout South Dakota, occupied the Gordon city auditorium, drew in television reporters, and received a couple of pages of coverage in *Life* magazine. No one had ever seen Indians behave like this in a border town.

Two of the perpetrators of the crime against Yellow Thunder, Les and Pat Hare, were found guilty of manslaughter and false imprisonment (Nebraska's term for restraining an individual against his will—a lesser charge than kidnapping) after a sensational trial in Alliance, Nebraska. AIM was there too, making its presence known to the judge and jury. For decades Indian victims of white crimes in the Nebraska border towns had received little justice. Now, everyone on the South Dakota reservations knew of AIM.

After the Yellow Thunder trial the movement joined the Trail of Broken Treaties, a protest march across America that ended in Washington, D.C., with the occupation of the Bureau of Indian Affairs (BIA) building for nine days in November 1972. A few months later it was Custer, South Dakota's turn. The town, nestled in the Black Hills, was named after one of the Lakotas' most hated enemies, Lieutenant Colonel George Armstrong Custer, whose Seventh Cavalry had been decimated by Lakota and Cheyenne at Little Big Horn in June 1876.

On January 21, 1973, two locals, Darld Schmitz, a white man, and Wesley Bad Heart Bull, an Oglala Lakota, engaged in a drunken brawl outside a bar in the hamlet of Buffalo Gap, South Dakota. Bad Heart Bull had attacked an employee with a chain and knocked him out, and Schmitz joined the ensuing melee. He stabbed Bad Heart Bull in the chest with a pocket knife. Hours later, the Indian died in a Rapid City hospital. Schmitz was charged with manslaughter. After pleas from Bad Heart Bull's mother to intervene, AIM took up the cause and, similar to the Yellow Thunder case, demanded that the charges be increased to murder.

AIM leaders were convinced by a private investigator's evidence that Schmitz was "hunting

Indians" that night, which would make the killing premeditated. They announced that AIM members would converge on the Custer courthouse on February 6 to present the organization's case to the authorities. As Means and Banks discussed their evidence with a state's attorney in the courthouse, a scuffle began just outside the front door. Police poured down from the second floor, and a riot ensued. AIM members fought back, and the incident ended with two buildings afire, numerous injuries on both sides, and scores of arrests.

✳　✳　✳

At the 2012 conference it was standing room only in the tiny classroom when a fair-haired young academic named Justin Hammer presented his paper. A recent graduate of the Indian Studies program at the University of South Dakota, he had traveled the length of the state and put on a crisp, light-blue dress shirt and tie for the occasion. Originally from Rapid City, South Dakota, with roots in the nearby town of Custer, Hammer had titled his lecture "Race and Perception: The 1973 American Indian Movement Protest in Custer, SD."

As Hammer recounted the basic facts of the conflict at the Custer courthouse, Russell Means sat in the corner of his right eye. Means wore a

Former AIM leader Russell Means and wife Pearl

black cowboy hat, a black shirt offset by a strand of bright turquoise beads, matching earrings, and a suit coat. Leather straps with silver studs flowed down from both sides of his head, replacing the braided ponytails he had most likely lost during his recent bout with cancer. Before his illness Means had been a large, muscular man with a potbelly that only added to his imposing stature; but the fight against esophageal cancer had taken its toll. He was becoming a frail old man.

Means had achieved recognition as one of the nation's last great orators in a time when most people had forgotten what an orator was. A tumor in his throat was tantamount to Van Clyburn losing both hands in a car accident. Sitting to Means's left was his wife, Pearl, and in the far corner, behind the young lecturer, sat one of Means's closest friends, the controversial left-wing academic Ward Churchill.

Means sat quietly through the presentation. But the quiet did not last long. He was listening to a man who was far less than half his age talking about an incident that Means had lived through.

Means was the product of twentieth-century government policies that many thought were designed to destroy Native American culture. His father, Hank, an Oglala from Pine Ridge, and his mother, Theodora, a Yankton, were graduates of

Indian boarding schools where teachers punished children who spoke anything but English. The schools sought to wipe Native culture from the minds of the children. Neither of his parents knew the Lakota language, so neither did Russell.

Hank and Theodora hated reservation life, and when World War II broke out they moved to the San Francisco Bay area to take advantage of the boom in defense industry jobs. But Means did not lose his connection to South Dakota. As a child he returned often to visit relatives. Increasingly, his visits were designed to keep him out of trouble in the big city. In high school Means got involved in drugs and graduated to the life of a small-time dealer. When the San Leandro police drummed him out of town, he drifted to Los Angeles where he began the first of several families.

In addition to restrictive schooling, federal policy also helped destroy Native culture through relocation. The Bureau of Indian Affairs paid families to move off impoverished reservations and into the cities. But there they could find only dead-end jobs and try to make their way in a foreign culture. In southern California, Means met relocated Native Americans from all over the country and from many different tribes. For the next fifteen years he drifted around the United States, working at a variety of jobs and sporadically attending colleges without ever coming close to earning a degree. After being fired from a job as an anti-poverty program administrator in the Rosebud Reservation in South Dakota, he applied for relocation and moved his family to Cleveland, Ohio. There he took his first steps toward activism when he formed an Indian Center to help relocated Native American families.

Means's work drew attention, and he dipped his toe into national waters, looking into organizations that sought to work within the white man's system to advance Native American causes. At a meeting of one of these groups he met AIM founders Banks and Bellecourt. He was initially taken aback by the two Ojibwes who were dressed, he thought quite inappropriately, in Native garb—beads, moccasins, and such. The pair were aggressively pushing a different, in-your-face activism that rubbed elders the wrong way. Means first derided the movement, but he soon gave himself over to it. With a knack for public speaking, he became its most charismatic and recognizable leader, and for a short time its national president.

If Means had nine lives like a cat, probably he had used eight of them during run-ins with rivals and the police in the 1970s. By the summer of 2011 it looked as if he might be well on his way to using up his ninth. After the cancer diagnosis, he announced that he would forgo Western medicine and treat the disease with Native remedies. His once-clear voice, which had enraptured his followers in rousing speeches without the need of a microphone, had been reduced to a rasp. Yet in the spring of 2012 Means announced that he had beaten the disease—with a mixture of traditional and Western treatments, he admitted. He carried a blue-and-white water bottle to combat a dry mouth, but his voice was back.

Justin Hammer's presentation did not go down well with Means. He had always disliked anthropologists. According to his autobiography, his grandmother first told him to avoid "anthros" when he was six years old. As an adult he observed them swarming over the reservations every summer, funded by grants and out to make a name for themselves by studying Indians like animals in a zoo. Their chief concern, "aside from furthering their careers," he wrote, "is to put Indians under a microscope, to reduce the people whose lives they study to objects instead of treating them like human beings." So when Hammer was introduced as an anthropology student, the Q&A session that followed his paper was bound to elicit a response from Means.

"I got something to say. I was there," he said, sitting forward in his chair. "I was involved at the time. The mother of Bad Heart Bull came to the American Indian Movement and asked for something to be done about the murder of her son. She didn't feel that her son was getting justice."

Means told how AIM had hired a private investigator from Minneapolis who found two white witnesses to the incident. They said that Schmitz had bragged earlier in the evening that he was going hunting for an Indian. That would possibly make the case premeditated, Means said. "I'm surprised you didn't bring this up . . ."

Hammer tried to respond: "I heard that but I was never able to validate it, so I—"

"Well, we did."

"And I—"

"Now hang on. You had your goddam time. Now listen to me," Means said, raising his voice for the first time. Someone in the audience said there was no call for that kind of language.

"It's your language," Means said. "You don't want to hear it, you shouldn't have taught it to me!"

Means went on to recount his memories of the riot: While the state's attorney refused to budge on the manslaughter charges, the mood among AIM supporters outside the courthouse grew tense. When Bad Heart Bull's mother tried to enter the building, she was manhandled. Shortly thereafter, state patrolmen dressed in full riot gear came streaming down from the second floor of the courthouse, igniting the riot. Who started the violence had been a matter of debate for thirty-nine years. Means maintained that the Indians were ambushed.

"The cops had her [the mother] and had already torn her blouse. It was snowing. She didn't have a jacket on. I don't know, they must have took it off her. And that was the mother of the man who had been killed. You don't do that!"

"And I had that included in my overall—" Hammer spurted, trying to explain that he couldn't give all the details of a ninety-seven-page thesis in a twenty-minute session. But Means wouldn't let him respond. "Hang on now. So all of a sudden from upstairs and downstairs came the helmeted police. . . . They had vigilantes. They made me sit in tear gas. And that's on film. The Custer vigilantes had me in a circle. They were begging the sheriff to let them have me for overnight. They almost acquiesced. If there wasn't highway patrol there, they probably would have. . . ."

During his presentation, Hammer had observed that the residents of Custer he interviewed for his research didn't believe they were racially prejudiced. Of course, few people believe they are prejudiced, or will admit it to someone with a tape recorder. But Means took Hammer's finding to mean that the residents of South Dakota were not in fact prejudiced.

"Now, I want to say something about your preface about racism in South Dakota," Means said. "Evidently you didn't play high school basketball, and if you did, you're oblivious. You don't know anything that goes on in that high school athletic association up in Pierre. The other thing is, you never rodeoed. I know there is racism in South Dakota . . ."

"I'm not denying there is racism in South Dakota . . ."

". . . and it is manifest. I challenge you to go sit in a Rapid City courtroom every morning. Do it for a couple of weeks. Count how many white guys or white women are in there. You won't even fill up one hand."

The moderator broke in: "In fairness to our other speakers, we have to move along. Thank you for contributing that. Are there any other questions?"

"Now wait a minute." Means wouldn't be silenced. "If you got time for other questions, I want to finish. Because he had his presentation.

You understand? Now you be polite. Because I'm not through with this man, because he just took nothing but white information and presented a racist presentation here. . . ."

"I used your book," Hammer said. "I used Ward Churchill's book. I've used Dennis Banks's book . . ."

"Well, you should have put it in your presentation then."

"I did have Dennis Banks in there and I had other—"

"Dennis Banks!" Means said derisively. The two leaders had been at odds for decades.

Hammer tried to get in the last word: "We're trying to get to a point. We are trying to get to a place where we can all live in South Dakota happily together, where race isn't a problem. It still is a problem in South Dakota."

"Then stop the racist presentations," Means said.

"I'm sorry but I don't—"

The moderator cut Hammer off.

THE OCCUPATION

Twenty-one days after the Custer courthouse riot, two FBI agents in an unmarked sedan followed a long string of cars leaving the Pine Ridge Reservation town of Calico. As the convoy headed east in the midwinter darkness, the G-men had to wonder where all these angry, radical Indians were going. The Bureau of Indian Affairs offices in Pine Ridge was the obvious answer, but the cavalcade sped by those well-guarded buildings in the town—flipping off the U.S. marshals manning their posts—and continued along Highway 18. As the agents radioed in the cars' movements to a command post, more vehicles were creeping up behind them to join the others. Suddenly they weren't following the convoy anymore, they were smack-dab in the middle of it. They turned north toward the towns of Porcupine and Kyle, came over a ridge, and saw the lead cars come to a stop at a cluster of houses in a valley. They swerved onto the shoulder to let the others pass.

The destination was the Wounded Knee settlement. It was February 27, 1973, and the occupation had begun.

AIM leaders, including Means, Banks, and Clyde Bellecourt, and their Lakota supporters had met earlier in the evening at the community hall in Calico. They were frustrated because they had made no headway in wresting control of the tribal government from its president, Dick Wilson. By the 1970s the Pine Ridge Reservation, spread out over some 3,500 square miles in the southwest corner of South Dakota, was well on its way to becoming the most impoverished area in the United States. Its society had become divided into two classes: the "traditionals" tried to maintain the old ways of life while the "nontraditionals" were more in tune with the white ways of doing things. Often, but not always, this attitude reflected blood quantum. The full-bloods tended to live in the countryside and had stronger ties to the land. The mixed-bloods congregated in the town of Pine Ridge and held a stranglehold on political power and lucrative tribal or federal jobs—just about the only kind of job to be found on the reservation. When AIM first came to Pine Ridge in 1972 to protest Yellow Thunder's death, they pitted themselves squarely against the newly elected, no-nonsense, crew-cut, right-wing, hippy-hating, plumber-turned-politician Wilson.

The first act of AIM-related violence on the reservation had taken place the preceding year in Wounded Knee. On the way back from Yellow Thunder's second interment following a second autopsy, some rank-and-file members broke off and headed for the trading post. A rumor had circulated that a boy had been assaulted there after being caught stealing. At the store the mourners confronted the longtime store owner, Clive Gildersleeve, and his business partner, Jim Czywczynski, threatening the two men. Then they did a smash-and-grab in the museum next door and sped away with several artifacts. The incident reportedly enraged Wilson.

The following year saw an influx of U.S. marshals, FBI agents, and Bureau of Indian Affairs police, there at the request of the local government and all clearly siding with the Wilson administration against the "radical Indians." And Wilson organized his own parapolice force, the Guardians of the Oglala Nation, or Goons, a nickname they embraced. AIM-friendly councilmen from the Pine Ridge rural districts attempted to impeach the tribal president, but without success. The traditionals accused him of thuggery and political intimidation. Wilson's bellicose rhetoric, aimed at his political opponents, seemed to back up these claims.

At the Calico meeting, AIM and Pine Ridge residents decided that more drastic measures should be taken. And so they set out for Wounded Knee.

Means had sent a vanguard to secure the village. By the time he arrived, the looting of the trading post and museum was well under way. He attempted, but failed, to stop it before going to the top of the hill to seize the highest point in the valley and take hostage the priest, Father Paul Manhart. When Manhart was bound, Means got on the only working telephone to call the media.

The protesters took twelve hostages, most of them elderly. After smashing the streetlights, the Vietnam vets among them set up a perimeter. Adrienne Fritze, a raven-haired, fair-skinned girl of twelve, was settling in for the night when she first heard shouting and gunshots. She lived in a mobile home next to the trading post with her parents, Jeanne and Guy, and her paraplegic maternal grandfather, Wilbur Riegert, who was Agnes Gildersleeve's brother. Jeanne Fritze had convinced her husband to move to South Dakota from their home in Virginia after Guy retired from the navy, so that she could care for her aging father.

Jim Czywczynski and his wife, Jan, who had bought a controlling interest in the trading post and were now running the store, were at a basketball game that evening.

Jeanne Fritze hustled Adrienne into the bathroom with the family dog and some quilts for added protection, and ordered her to lay low in the bathtub to protect herself from stray bullets. But as soon as her mother left, Adrienne couldn't resist peeping through the window at the scene outside. A group of men were swarming the village; some had looted the trading post and now carried hunting rifles that were sold there. Others were shooting out streetlights. And then the young men converged on the mobile home, and Adrienne ducked down as her mother had instructed.

One man smashed the back-door window and demanded that Jeanne open it. "You already broke the window. Reach in and open it yourself!" she shouted, standing back.

The men burst through the door, spouting foul language and brandishing knives and guns as the family was herded into a single room. There they were held hostage along with the Gildersleeves, Father Manhart, and Agnes's sister, Mary. The following day they were shuffled from home to home. Adrienne was not permitted to leave the house as armed guards kept a constant vigil.

The Gildersleeves by that time had lived at Wounded Knee for almost forty years. Agnes was a mixed-blood Ojibwe from Minnesota and a distant cousin of the Bellecourt brothers, Clyde and Vern. She had first come to work at Pine Ridge as a clerk for the Bureau of Indian Affairs. Clive was a second-generation white trader. He had inherited the business from his father and had lived on Pine Ridge his entire life. Agnes's brother Wilbur Riegert worked as a BIA accountant. The trading post served the residents of the small village that had grown up around the massacre site. Wounded Knee had mostly disappeared from public consciousness in the decades after the Seventh Cavalry gunned down approximately 150 men, women, and children in 1890. For a few years the nearby settlement was officially called Brennan, after a white Indian agent, in an effort to erase the memory of what had happened there.

In the late 1960s Clive Gildersleeve, Jim Czywczynski, and other business partners wanted to build a truly massive memorial on the hill where the victims were buried, a structure that would resemble those on the National Mall in Washington, D.C. They looked for white investors from Rapid City and never consulted with tribal elders. They even made a play to wrest control of the burial site's land from the Holy Rosary Mission. The ultimate goal was to build hotels and other tourist-related businesses similar to those in the nearby Black Hills. The controversial project never materialized, but it damaged the Gildersleeve family's reputation. To AIM, the family was attempting to cash in on the massacre's increasing notoriety.

Some residents complained that the Gildersleeves' trading post prices were higher, but the post was not like the big grocery stores in town that could sell in volume. It extended credit to those in need and sometimes bartered beadwork and art for food. When a customer needed to borrow a phone, or needed a ride into town in an emergency, Clive and Agnes helped. Most of their customers they had known their whole lives. Czywczynski, however, was an outsider to reservation life and a hard-nosed businessman. He lacked the Gildersleeves' empathy and knowledge of the local culture and rubbed some customers the wrong way.

Wilbur Riegert, eighty-two years old, had amassed a collection of art and relics, and kept them in a museum next to the trading post; but he was hardly growing rich off the admission fees. When he first came to the reservation as a young man to work as a BIA accountant, he had met the Lakota physician George Eastman, a key figure from the 1890 massacre who had treated many of its survivors. The encounter had a profound affect on Riegert's life. Although he had Ojibwe blood in him, he became enamored with Lakota culture and history, and produced an illustrated self-published book, *I Am a Sioux Indian*, which he sold to visitors. An old baseball injury had caught up with him in his later years and put him in a wheelchair. Still, he spent his days at the museum, telling visitors all he knew about Lakota culture and history. As the occupation began, he witnessed his life's work being taken away piece by piece.

At first the families certainly were held against their will. Adrienne, eavesdropping on a discussion among senior AIM leaders, heard at least one of them tell the others that keeping elderly hostages, including one wheelchair-bound man and a girl, would not win any sympathy for their cause. The Gildersleeves, however, were uncertain about leaving. When she had the opportunity, Agnes at times told the FBI that she was being treated as a prisoner. At other times she said that she and her husband didn't want to leave; they would rather stay and keep an eye on their property.

Outside the village, FBI Special Agent in Charge Joe Trimbach set up roadblocks. Trimbach, by his own admission, was clearly in over his head. He had been head of FBI operations in Minnesota and North and South Dakota for less than a month. He knew next to nothing about Native American culture and history and the internal dynamics of the reservation that were driving the occupation. He also knew little about the strengths and weaknesses of the men under his command. The Justice Department was nominally in charge, but turf battles immediately broke out between the FBI, the U.S. Marshals Service, the Bureau of Indian Affairs, the Justice Department, and army advisers. The marshals' director, Wayne Colburn, flew in from Washington to take charge of his men on the scene. As the head of a Justice Department agency, he seemingly outranked Trimbach and tried to show it. But the special agent in charge refused to put his men and women under Colburn's command. In one instance Trimbach also had to muzzle Dick Wilson, who was threatening to lead his Goons on an assault of the village. Trimbach saw the feds as the only force standing between the two sides. Meanwhile both he and Colburn allowed armed Goons—some of them teenagers, barely old enough to shave—to operate freely outside the sealed-off village.

Trimbach's agents were given high-powered rifles and armored personnel carriers, and told to man checkpoints. Questionable orders came from Washington to "shoot-to-wound," not kill. But FBI agents were not soldiers or snipers, they were investigators. How could an agent—untrained with such weapons—fire with precision from hundreds of yards away? Trimbach saw it as his duty not only to keep the AIM protesters inside Wounded Knee but also to handle the media onslaught and the negotiations with the hostage takers.

The armored personnel carriers formed a ring around the valley. Behind the scenes, army officers were advising the FBI and the marshals, maintaining the vehicles, and later arranging for air force surveillance aircraft to fly over and take pictures of the Wounded Knee defenses. Trimbach knew next to nothing about the historical significance of Wounded Knee and could not fathom why the army wouldn't want to call up its civil disturbance unit, take charge, and clear out the occupiers. Pentagon leaders apparently knew how bad that would look, and they declined to authorize any such operation. The Nixon administration agreed.

Means, Banks, Bellecourt, and the occupiers, many of them women and children, meanwhile found themselves surrounded by hostiles as their names and faces were splashed across front pages throughout the world.

Banks, along with Means, emerged as one of the chief spokesmen. Like the Bellecourt brothers, he was an Ojibwe from Minnesota, but he hailed from the Leech Lake Reservation. As a boy, he was torn apart from his family and spent eleven years in Indian boarding schools in North and South Dakota. The institutions were notorious for their cruel treatment, and curricula designed to erase Native culture and languages from their wards. After a stint in the air force, he drifted around Minnesota, until he was arrested and sent to jail on burglary charges. While imprisoned, he began reconnecting to his native culture, and took advantage of the prison library, where he studied the tactics of black civil rights activists. Almost as soon as his eighteen-month sentence was completed in 1968, he was ready to devote his life to the cause. It didn't take him long to connect with Clyde Bellecourt.

Among the other notable protest leaders were Vietnam War veterans Carter Camp and Stan Holder, who headed the security details; Leonard Crow Dog, a medicine man from the neighboring Rosebud Reservation; and the Oglala leader of the anti-Wilson Oglala Sioux Civil Rights Organization, Pedro Bissonette.

✳   ✳   ✳

The time was right for an uprising. After the conclusion of the so-called Indian Wars in the nineteenth century, Native Americans found themselves mostly put away on reservations. By the mid-twentieth century they existed as cartoonish stereotypes in television shows and movies, where they were usually portrayed as the bad guys—the "savages" out to scalp the poor pioneers. For the general public, the fate of the continent's first peoples was out of sight, out of mind. Federal policies such as termination, which eliminated federal recognition of some tribes, and relocation, described earlier, were designed to absolve the government of its obligations. The Dawes Allotment Act, imposed on the Lakotas and many other tribes against their will in 1887, gave 160 acres of land to each head of an Indian household. The law's stated goal was to force the Indians to adopt the white man's ways by becoming farmers. But after only a few generations, most of this prime cattle-grazing land and farmland on Pine Ridge was being leased out to white ranchers or owned by white men married to Native women or mixed-bloods. The Oglalas had one of the largest reservations in America, but they saw little benefit from the one thing that gave their white neighbors their wealth: the land itself.

The typical Oglala family at the beginning of the century had a garden, some cattle and horses, and a few chickens. Each year they did some labor in the border communities, harvesting potatoes and sugar beets to earn extra money. They had some annual government rations in the form of flour, sugar, and coffee, but for the most part they were self-sufficient. Some Lakota men went off to fight in World War I and returned only to find that white ranchers' cattle had overrun their farms and that their land had been taken away for failure to pay property taxes. Children were sent to schools where they were physically punished for speaking their Native language. Traditional religious ceremonies such as the Sun Dance were banned.

In Lakota society no chiefs held absolute power; decisions were made by discussion among the elders. But Congress imposed democracy on Indian tribes in 1935 under the Indian Reform Act. Consensus building among the traditional leaders was scrapped in favor of the election of tribal chairmen. Mixed-blood Oglalas who knew how to play the game seized control of the local government, set their relatives up with jobs, and marginalized the traditionals. Meanwhile a white bureaucrat sent to Pine Ridge in the form of a superintendent was looking over their shoulder and could negate any laws—especially if they were considered detrimental to the white ranchers or farmers who lived on the reservation. By 1973, if an Oglala on Pine Ridge didn't have a government job, he or she was most likely on welfare. The Great Society ensured that the Indians had enough to eat, but that was about it. Alcoholism, poverty, and hopelessness became epidemic.

The average American may have had some knowledge of the nineteenth-century Indian Wars, and maybe even realized that Native Americans had received a raw deal back then. But most knew next to nothing about how U.S. government policies imposed in the twentieth century had transformed self-sufficient peoples into wards of the state and the beautiful lands they lived on—the reservations—into rural ghettos. This story had not been told.

*   *   *

Early on at Wounded Knee, the 1973 occupiers assumed that their days were numbered and that the feds would come over the hill to invade at any moment. The hostages provided at least some assurance that there wouldn't be a second bloodbath on this same site.

Into this situation stepped the state's two U.S. senators, James Abourezk and George McGovern, both Democrats. Abourezk had been in office only seven weeks but certainly knew the lay of the land. He had grown up near the neighboring

Rosebud Reservation. At the turn of the twentieth century, when a small stream of Christians
from present-day Lebanon made their way to
the American heartland, his father, Beshara Abu
Rizk, was among them. He anglicized his name,
changing it to Charles Thomas Abourezk, and
made his living walking between remote settler
homes on the Northern prairie with a backpack
of goods. The backpack soon became a horse and
buggy, the horse and buggy became a car. And
when the roads improved Abourezk gave up his
life as an itinerant peddler and opened a store on
the edge of the Rosebud Reservation in Wood,
South Dakota. His son James grew up multicul-
tural before there was such a word. At home his
mother spoke Arabic. Lakotas from the Brule
tribe traded with his father, and a few lived in the
tiny town of Wood, which had once been part of
the reservation but had been taken away in a land
grab. The settlers and their children came from
all walks of life—American Easterners, Scandi-
navian or Western European immigrants—all
there to make a go of homesteading in the semi-
arid land.

James grew up in Wood during the Great De-
pression and the Dust Bowl. The plight of Native
Americans made little impression on him at first.
As a young man he ridiculed the alcoholics who

hung around Wood and bought lemon or vanilla extract from his father in order to get drunk.

After serving in the navy, Abourezk married and started a family as he went from job to job, mostly bartending in rough-and-tumble South Dakota watering holes. He wanted a better life, so he pursued higher education, first earning a degree in civil engineering, then eventually going into law and setting up a practice in Rapid City. By this time he had shed the prejudices of his youth and had become a champion for the state's Native Americans, who had been living under a dual standard of justice for years. He began working cases *pro bono* for the American Civil Liberties Union and became more heavily involved in the Democratic party, which had little support in deeply conservative western South Dakota. Nonetheless he was elected to the U.S. House of Representatives in 1971 and won the Senate seat in November 1972.

Abourezk's involvement in the Wounded Knee occupation began when a staff member told him that protesters had taken over the village. Not sure of what to do, he found a South Dakota phone book and called a random number for a residence in Wounded Knee. It turned out to be the house that Means and Banks had converted into a makeshift headquarters. Means, whom Abourezk had known for years, came to the phone.

Means informed him that the protesters had taken over Wounded Knee, were holding hostages, and would not release them unless Abourezk came there to negotiate—along with Secretary of State Henry Kissinger and Senators William Fulbright and Ted Kennedy. Abourezk immediately called the two senators, who were not interested, but they promised to send one staffer each. When he told Means that he did not call Kissinger, Means demanded that Nixon's counsel John Ehrlichman come instead. Abourezk said he wasn't about to ride in an airplane for three hours with one of Nixon's thugs. Means acquiesced and said that once the retinue arrived, the protesters would release the hostages.

Abourezk did convince McGovern to come with him. The senior senator from South Dakota had been on the short end of one of the worst landslides in presidential history the previous fall. The two lawmakers and the congressional staffers hopped an air force flight going to Ellsworth Air Force Base, near Rapid City, then boarded a helicopter to Pine Ridge.

Trimbach was there to greet them. Abourezk told him to inform Means of their arrival and see that the hostages were released as promised. The two senators were left to cool their heels in Pine Ridge for three hours, waiting for word from the occupied village. Abourezk finally decided they should just go in by themselves. They found a car, tied a white piece of cloth to it, and slowly drove into the valley. There they were surrounded by mean-looking armed men who gave them the stink eye. McGovern turned to Abourezk and asked, "Jim, why did you have to be so damned courageous?"

After hours of negotiations, Abourezk believed he had a deal in place for the protesters to release the hostages and leave the village. Privately, Means's only demands were that they be told how high their bail would be after submitting to arrest. Abourezk flew back to Washington believing the wheels for a settlement were in motion. He was wrong: the occupation would continue for another sixty-nine days.

For Adrienne Fritze, the most traumatic day of the siege at Wounded Knee occurred when she saw one of the occupiers riding and whipping her beloved horse Ginger. Adrienne had suffered sexual abuse by her father, and Ginger was her refuge. She had raised her from a colt after the horse was born in the village.

Adrienne went into hysterics and bolted out of the trailer home wailing. That startled the armed guards outside, and she heard the mechanical sounds of rounds being chambered. "Don't shoot her, don't shoot her, don't shoot her!" Means cried. She heard him running behind her, but he wasn't fast enough. She dashed toward her horse screaming. Other occupiers finally caught up with her. Means turned her around, assuring her that everything would be okay, and ordered the young man off the horse. He had Ginger tied up outside where Adrienne could see her. Adrienne sat at the kitchen table the rest of the day, keeping watch on Ginger until the sun went down and she couldn't keep her eyes open any longer. When she awoke the next day, the mare was gone. She would never see her again.

On another day, when all the adults decided to meet, they told Adrienne to go into the living room. One young guard volunteered to watch her. Clive Gildersleeve was there too. By then her great-uncle seemed to be reduced to a shell. He was utterly defeated and spent his time gazing out a window. The guard approached her and drew her into a shadow. He grabbed her, rubbed up against her. As a victim of her father, she knew what was happening and escaped his clutches by stepping into the light. The molester lost his nerve and let her go.

By March 8 all the hostages had been released, probably because AIM leaders were worried about bad publicity. The captives had watched helplessly as occupiers stole their personal property with impunity. Just about anything of value that could be carried out was taken right before their eyes, and they could do nothing about it. Jeanne Fritze saw women walking around in her clothes. Wilbur Riegert was heartbroken beyond words—his museum was destroyed. (He would not live long enough to hear AIM leaders tell gullible historians that his museum set out to glorify the massacre at Wounded Knee and deride its victims.) Agnes Gildersleeve complained to Banks about a family heirloom clock someone had stolen; he got it back for her. Otherwise everything was gone. The occupiers allowed her one truck to carry off the belongings that remained. March 8 was the last day the Gildersleeves would spend in their home.

With the hostages out, the only thing standing between the hundreds of FBI agents, marshals, BIA police, and Wilson's Goons was the thought of a second Wounded Knee massacre at the hands of the government. Carter Camp and

Stan Holder had rounded up all the occupiers with military experience and begun constructing bunkers. They had their own hunting rifles, a few taken from the trading post, and limited ammunition. More would be smuggled in.

The feds used the armored personnel carriers for cover as they formed a ring around the bowl-shaped valley. The firefights began in earnest later in March. Throughout the occupation there would be several intense battles. The two federal agencies and the Goons poured hundreds of thousands of rounds into the Wounded Knee fortifications and buildings.

Along with removing Wilson, the protesters' demands were many and were chosen for publicity's sake more than practicality. Means, Bissonette, and others had gone out to meet Trimbach the first morning of the occupation to demand that the Treaty of 1868, which granted large swaths of land to the Lakotas, be recognized and enforced, that the sacred Black Hills be returned to the Lakotas, and that a congressional hearing be held to examine the nation's compliance with all 371 treaties it had signed with Native American tribes. The AIM leaders wanted an independent Oglala Nation too. The demands were never met.

Justice Department mediators and AIM leaders negotiated several cease-fires, but they were all broken. In most cases, each side accused the other of firing the first shots. In one battle on March 23, some two thousand rounds were fired by the two sides. Despite all the lead flying about, no one was hurt. Three days later, during another furious exchange, that luck ran out. Lloyd Grimm, a marshal who had been pulling desk duty at the town of Pine Ridge, came out to see the occupied village for the first time. A firefight erupted, and Grimm was struck in the chest from a bullet fired from an AIM-occupied bunker. The slug made a ricochet off his rib cage and severed his spine. He would remain in a wheelchair the rest of his life.

Daily life inside the village was becoming a struggle for the occupiers. Food, clothing, and medicine were often in short supply. But some of the participants found life inside Wounded Knee exhilarating. Crow Dog conducted traditional religious ceremonies and built a sweat lodge, insisting that all newcomers go inside to be purified. Many said they felt free to be Indians for the first time in their lives—despite being surrounded by hostile government forces. When AIM sent out a call for supporters, food, and ammunition, left-wing organizations answered it. Supplies were stockpiled in safe havens in Rapid City, Pine Ridge, and the nearby Rosebud

Reservation. Those who sneaked past the feds' gauntlet backpacked in as much as they could carry.

Celebrities and sympathizers began gravitating to the village. Civil rights leader Ralph Abernathy made it inside, as did dozens of other Native Americans and activists who wanted to lend their support. One was Anna Mae Pictou, a Canadian from the Mi'kmaq tribe and mother of two, and her soon-to-be second husband, Nogeeshik Aquash, an Ojibwe. They held their wedding ceremony inside the village in full view of the press. Another woman bore a child during the occupation.

But each new sympathizer—Native American, white, Chicano, or black—was another mouth to feed. Those the AIM leaders didn't trust were sent packing. Some grew tired of the austere conditions and firefights and left on their own. Even more were intercepted by the feds before they arrived, arrested, and sent to Rapid City jails. This brought in a cadre of out-of-state, left-leaning attorneys—veterans of the 1960s civil rights movement, including Mark Lane and William Kunstler—who had experience in going toe-to-toe with federal and establishment judges. They would play a prominent role in the trials resulting from the occupation.

Meanwhile the FBI, the Goons, and the marshals did their best to keep the media out. Despite Trimbach's efforts, reporters at first had almost unfettered access to the occupied village. There to give them an education on the mistreatment of Native Americans were Means, Banks, and Bellecourt. The images of freedom fighters defying the mighty United States government were transmitted around the world. The leaders' fiery rhetoric was always quotable.

The location was, after all, genius. The book *Bury My Heart at Wounded Knee* had recently spent months as the country's No. 1 nonfiction best-seller. In it author Dee Brown spelled out the injustices perpetrated on Native Americans in the nineteenth century. Now, here was a group pointing out injustices in the twentieth century—and at the very same place noted in the book's title. Moreover the main spokesman was the always quotable Russell Means. Telegenic, intelligent, and media-savvy, both he and Banks were quickly becoming household names. Their defiant anti-Wilson act had morphed into a symbolic protest against the horrors visited upon America's first peoples. From deliberate acts of genocide and culture-cide to the corrupt and inept Bureau of Indian Affairs, the grievances were many and legitimate. As the cameras rolled and reporters jotted down the words of Means and Banks, the federal government never got its act together to counter AIM's message. To most of the world, the protesters were freedom fighters. To the FBI, they were criminals.

As a symbolic place to occupy, Wounded Knee was a powerful choice. As a spot for the protesters to defend, it could have been a catastrophe. Except for the small bump on the land where the church and mass grave were located, the AIM occupiers found themselves in a giant bowl which the feds could easily surround and attack from higher ground.

As weeks passed, the feds did a better job of intercepting supplies, and there was less and less food for the occupiers to share with their supporters. Local cattle that strayed too close to the valley were "captured," slaughtered, and eaten. That may have been Ginger's fate as well. On two occasions, sympathizers flew supplies in. One pilot organized an airdrop. Another actually landed as the marshals shot at his aircraft.

Informants working for the FBI or the marshals also infiltrated the occupiers. It was all too easy for spies to pose as sympathizers, and AIM leadership knew it. Trimbach, during his two weeks at Wounded Knee, requested a legal wiretap on the one phone line leading into the village. This was denied since the phone was being used for client-attorney communications. But a tap was installed under his watch anyway—illegally.

As AIM leaders grew more concerned about informants, they interrogated Al Cooper, a white veteran of the 1960s civil rights movement, at gunpoint. Cooper's roots as an activist went back further than the AIM leaders, and he had been in the village since the second week, but he suddenly found himself chained to a bed and surrounded by Holder and Crow Dog. After intense questioning, they decided to let him go. As he returned to the bunker shaken and shocked, he had no idea what had brought on this sudden accusation.

As it turned out, the grilling has been prompted by the arrival of an acquaintance, Perry Ray Robinson. Both men were veterans of the 1964 Albany (Georgia) City Jail hunger strikes. In 1962 Martin Luther King, Jr., and his followers had waged a war of wills with Albany sheriff Laurie Pritchett and lost. Pritchett had studied King's nonviolent tactics and devised a strategy to counter them: he would meet nonviolence with nonviolent incarceration. No barking dogs or fire hoses, just nonstop arrests until the marchers' spirits were broken. Two years after King had left Albany in defeat, activists on a Canada-to-Cuba peace march attempted to walk though downtown carrying pacifist slogans. But Pritchett would have none of that. He threw them in jail and had the local judge sentence them for thirty to forty days. Some thirty-five marchers were incarcerated six to a cell built for two, infested with cockroaches, with dirty windows overlooking an alleyway. The protesters responded with a hunger strike, which made some headlines. Supporters arrived from around the country and began their own hunger strike on the sidewalk outside the jail. Pritchett arrested them too.

Robinson was a former boxer. He lived in Washington, D.C., but had little direction in life when the protesters came though on their way to Cuba. He joined the march and threw himself into the cause. Also on the march was Barbara Deming, one of the intellectuals behind the pacifist movement. From her Robinson learned this new way of life. She would remember Robinson's efforts to keep up the protesters' spirits by singing to them from his own jail cell. Robinson was the first to declare that he would go without water as well as food.

The jailings and the hunger strike in Albany went largely unnoticed, which allowed Pritchett to impose punishments at will on the pacifists, including strapping Robinson to a chair and force-feeding him with cold, acidic orange juice.

After that ordeal ended, Robinson moved to Madison, Wisconsin, where the Committee to End the War in Vietnam hired him to organize the black community against the war. It was there that he met and fell in love with fellow activist and teacher Cheryl Buswell. They married and eventually settled on a farm near Selma, Alabama, where the two grew food for the local Black Panther party. They had three children together, Desi, Deeter, and Tamara. Their activist life was moderating as they began to raise their kids as well as the crops. But Robinson heard AIM's call for supporters at Wounded Knee and decided to answer it—over Cheryl's objections.

Cooper had not seen Robinson since Albany and was happy to greet him. They spoke briefly. National Public Radio reporter Kevin McKiernan, one of the last journalists to make it inside Wounded Knee, saw Robinson as well, though they did not speak.

The prevailing story is that Robinson clashed verbally with AIM members after his arrival. The pacifist ex-boxer found himself surrounded by Indian militants who were firing rifles at the enemy. A verbal spat, possibly over these tactics, escalated. One version of the story has him being ordered to meet with Banks, when a gun went off. The bullet pierced an artery in Robinson's leg, and he began to bleed out. He was taken to a makeshift infirmary but was never again seen alive.

Ironically, AIM leadership never ferreted out one of the most notorious FBI informants—Doug Durham, a white man posing as an Indian photojournalist, who arrived in Wounded Knee on March 20, took pictures of the fortifications, then shared them with the FBI. Over the next two years he was gradually allowed into Banks's inner circle and collected a thousand dollars a month from the FBI for his efforts.

✻   ✻   ✻

Wounded Knee initially made the front pages, but it had competition: in Washington the Watergate scandal was beginning to take a serious toll on the Nixon administration. For almost a year the White House had denied any involvement with the break-in and bugging of the Democratic National Committee office at the Watergate complex, but as the occupation at Wounded Knee dragged on, the administration began to unravel. Its attention was distracted.

After just two weeks of the occupation, the FBI brought in the no-nonsense veteran Special

Agent in Charge Roy Moore to relieve Trimbach. In retrospect Trimbach thought he had tried to do too much. Had J. Edgar Hoover been alive, Trimbach believed, the chief would never have allowed his agents to become involved in a paramilitary operation. He would have pulled them out. But Hoover had died in May 1972, less than a year earlier. Nor was it the FBI's job to handle negotiations or try to control the media; FBI personnel were supposed to be investigators. Moore disengaged his agents from those peripheral tasks and left them to the Justice Department.

His chain of command was in flux, to say the least. He answered to the acting director of the FBI, L. Patrick Gray, who answered to Attorney General Richard Kleindienst. Gray was a Nixon appointee who had the unenviable job of following one of the twentieth century's most powerful Washington figures. He resigned on April 28. His boss, Kleindienst, along with White House staffers John Ehrlichman and H.R. Haldeman, went with him.

At Wounded Knee there was no love lost between marshals and FBI agents. The marshals drew up plans—never executed—for a full-scale assault that would involve tear gas, armored personnel carriers, and deadly fire, but they didn't share them with the FBI. And neither agency had control over Wilson's Goons. Wilson continued to call press conferences, using anti-Communist rhetoric that by 1973 already seemed a bit anachronistic. His allegations that AIM was receiving direct support from Cuba and the Soviet Union would have made red-baiters such as Senator Joe McCarthy proud.

Late April 1973 was a turning point, punctuated by two deaths. A forty-seven-year-old man who claimed to be an Apache Indian made his way to Wounded Knee through the network of gullies in the middle of the night with his young, pregnant wife. On April 25 he was shot and killed during a firefight. AIM leaders insisted he was the Native American Frank Clearwater. But Wilson produced an FBI document that showed the man was Frank Clear, born in Virginia and dishonorably discharged from the army in World War II for fleeing in the face of the enemy during the Italian campaign. He was reportedly sleeping in one of the occupied homes hours after he arrived when a bullet came through the wall and struck him in the head. Who he was, what he was doing at Wounded Knee, and the circumstances surrounding his death remained murky.

Everyone knew Buddy Lamont, though. Born and raised on Pine Ridge, he was a Vietnam veteran who was flushed out of a bunker on April 26, the day the marshals first used tear gas. He was shot in the chest and died from his wound.

After the two deaths, morale inside the village ebbed: food was running out, supplies were low. The media, save for Kevin McKiernan, had disappeared, and the occupation was no longer making the front pages. Except for Dennis Banks, most of the leaders had departed. Means had left for the nation's capital, believing he would meet with important officials to discuss AIM's demands—but the talks never materialized. Clyde Bellecourt had gone to join his brother Vern in raising funds.

Two days after Lamont's death, a group of Lakota elders—acting as intermediaries between the occupiers and the Justice Department—negotiated an end to the occupation. That night the Wounded Knee trading post burned to the ground. Some say it was intentionally lit, other accounts called the fire an accident. Crow Dog and Camp were arrested and released on bond. Banks, who said he did not agree to the negotiated terms but would acquiesce to the elders' wishes, sneaked out of the village. Before the occupiers withdrew, the remaining buildings in the village were torched. All the artifacts in the museum had long been smuggled out.

Adrienne Fritze and her family had holed up in nearby Rushville, Nebraska, during the occupation. They came back to Wounded Knee only once, to assess the damage. It was complete. Everything they had was in ruins. The Fritzes moved to Rapid City to start over while the Gildersleeves spent their waning years living in poverty with relatives. Wilbur Riegert died about a year later. There was talk about the federal government compensating the families for their losses, but nothing came of it.

Today a smaller, steeple-less chapel stands near the mass grave at Wounded Knee. Beside it, Buddy Lamont rests alongside the victims of the 1890 massacre and other Wounded Knee residents who have died during the past thirty-nine years. The AIM-built bunkers have melted into the earth, leaving barely perceptible hollows. Tourists stop to see the so-called Last Battle of the Indian Wars, but few venture down the hill across the road to see the concrete foundation of the trading post. A chimney that was once in Riegert's museum is all that remains of the building. The foundations of other structures remain in the grass. The trading post's concrete floor is covered in shards of glass, the remnants of recent drinking sessions. Some say that nearby, in the gulley where the 1890 massacre victims once

gathered, Ray Robinson's body rests i[...]
grave, but that is pure conjecture. [...]
clandestine burials surfaced during the occupation, and the FBI scoured the nearby hills looking for fresh burial sites as soon as they retook the village. But they found nothing.

Means would one day write: "What Wounded Knee told the world was that John Wayne hadn't killed us all. Essentially, the rest of the planet had believed that except for a few people sitting along the highways peddling pottery, there were no more Indians. Suddenly, billions of people knew we were still alive, still resisting."

✳   ✳   ✳

The Center for Western Studies was crowded on Friday afternoon for the 3:50 p.m. panel, "Session 13: Revisiting Key Questions Concerning the 1973 Takeover and Occupation of Wounded Knee." As part of the conference, the organizers had pulled together an art exhibition, "Interpretations of Wounded Knee 1973 and 1890." Surrounding the speakers were poignant and angry paintings marking both the massacre and the seventy-one-day siege.

Joseph Trimbach walked in with a cane. He was now almost completely bald, his pate covered in brown age spots; the only remaining hairs on his head were the remnants of sideburns. Trimbach had been an ambitious up-and-comer in the FBI when AIM came to South Dakota. "Special Agent in Charge" was a big deal in the bureau: there were only a few of these Hoover lieutenants, and the position was almost as high as a rank-and-file agent could achieve. FBI agents in the Hoover era generally had two career paths. Field office special agents were usually family men who preferred to put down roots in one city and stay there for their entire career. And then there were those who chose to climb the ladder—their lives were similar to nomadic military officers. They pulled duty at FBI headquarters and various regional offices, and sometimes served overseas. Trimbach was one of those.

Most within the agency were charged, under the FBI's original intent, to pursue common criminals and mobsters who violated federal crimes or crossed state lines. Some agents were in counterespionage: they tracked foreign spies. And others had the job of monitoring citizens whom Hoover considered to be somehow anti-American—such as those who joined the Communist party in the depths of the Great Depression, which was not uncommon among the intelligentsia. By the 1950s the witch hunt for Communists was in full swing, thanks chiefly to Senator McCarthy, and

Hoover's FBI joined in. Many Americans' lives were ruined because of what they believed, or for attending a party meeting two decades in the past. In the 1960s Hoover turned his attention to anyone he thought was organizing counter to his sense of what a good American should think and do. The FBI became a tool of the right in its never-ending fight against the left (though violent extremist groups on the right, such as the Ku Klux Klan, were also included). FBI tactics included monitoring, wiretapping, and infiltrating nonviolent organizations, and disrupting their efforts to reach their political goals. If these groups crossed the line into violence or criminal activity, as AIM did, the FBI had all the cover it needed.

For seventeen years Trimbach climbed the FBI ladder, moving from post to post with his wife, Kathleen, and the family that would eventually grow to seven children. Occasionally he had a nerve-wracking audience with Hoover. Trimbach made a name for himself in Jacksonville, Florida, by busting corrupt local police. That earned him accolades from Hoover and Attorney General Robert F. Kennedy. When he was named Special Agent in Charge of the Minnesota and North and South Dakota region in the spring of 1973, he appeared to have made

it big. The position was important but compli-
cated. Not only was the territory large, it counted
twenty-one Indian reservations within the three
states. And the FBI had jurisdiction to investigate major crimes committed by Native Americans against Native Americans on reservations,
including murder, manslaughter, rape, assault
with intent to commit murder, arson, burglary,
and larceny. Minor crimes were left to tribal police and courts.

Trimbach knew next to nothing about the
Native peoples of the Northern plains. He hadn't
had a chance to warm his office chair in Minneapolis when he found himself in the thick of
an intertribal fight that had been ongoing for
more than a hundred years. The day he arrived
on the job he received a request from the Bureau
of Indian Affairs, via the Justice Department, to
go to Rapid City, South Dakota, and assist local
law enforcement in monitoring AIM in the aftermath of the Custer courthouse riot. That was
February 12, 1973.

Trimbach was on duty the night AIM and
its supporters occupied the village at Wounded
Knee. He spent just two weeks on the job before
higher-ups ordered him back to Minneapolis.
FBI insiders later told historian Rolland Dewing that Trimbach's zeal to investigate and arrest

AIM leaders led to his removal from the scene. Of course, that's really all an FBI agent of his day was trained to do. Nothing in the FBI manual explained how to surround a village with two hundred men, women, and children inside, some of them armed and shooting back at his agents.

Trimbach retired from the FBI in 1979, his once-promising career cut short. He was determined to spend his remaining years trying to get the convictions he believed the senior AIM leaders deserved. Although he lived in Florida, he had traveled to South Dakota in the 2000s

Former FBI Special Agent in Charge
Joseph Trimbach

to observe the trials of Arlo Looking Cloud and John Graham, two men convicted of murdering Anna Mae Aquash.

As Trimbach took a seat at the 2012 conference, the rotund Clyde Bellecourt and his younger friend Frank Paro, former chairman of AIM's Twin Cities chapter, sat down in the front row on the other side of the slide projector. They wore silky black AIM jackets. Bellecourt clutched two documents in his hand; over the next hour he would wield them like a weapon while anti-AIM speakers took center stage. One document included twenty-nine pages of prosecutorial misconduct compiled by AIM lawyers. The other was Judge Fred J. Nichol's memorandum explaining in detail why, on October 9, 1974, he dismissed the federal government's charges against Banks and Means following a sensational trial stemming from the occupation.

Bellecourt, by now seventy-five years old, had been hanging around the art gallery all morning, sitting on benches in the back of the room and waiting for the Trimbach-led panel to begin. He hailed from the Ojibwe's White Earth Reservation in Minnesota but had spent his formative years in St. Paul. His youth had been marked by a series of run-ins with the law and resulting prison sentences. It was during a stint in a state prison that he began to connect with his Native spiritual roots and to study more about his tribe's history. Once out of prison, he found his calling as an activist. He co-founded the American Indian Movement in 1968 with Dennis Banks as a means to combat police brutality and the dual standard of justice that existed in the Twin Cities. One of his first successful campaigns was to form groups that would attempt to tamp down trouble in the impoverished Indian neighborhoods before the police arrived. When arrests were made, the groups monitored the police to ensure that those apprehended had access to lawyers and weren't mistreated.

All this Friday morning, Means and Bellecourt had been in the Center's central hall where the panels took place, but they were not seen speaking together. Clyde and his late brother Vernon Bellecourt were longtime rivals of Means. Vern and Means especially had despised each other since the 1970s and until Vern's death in 2007. The four leaders, including Banks, had briefly worked together to march on the hamlet of Whiteclay, Nebraska, in the summer of 1999 in the wake of the murders of two Oglala men near the border; but it wasn't long afterward that Means accused the Bellecourts of ordering the murder of Aquash, whom they suspected of being an informant, and accused Banks of knowing about it after the fact but doing nothing.

Breaking from the norm, the conference organizer Harry Thompson took the podium to make an announcement. He looked and sounded like a high school principal cautioning a school assembly that was about to hear a lecture on sexually transmitted disease. This session "is of obvious interest to a number of people," Thompson intoned. "And we welcome that. We ask, as with all of our sessions, that you give the presenters the opportunity to express their opinions, present their research. There will be time for questions after their presentations. We ask that everyone be respectful. Please be in the spirit of education. This is an educational institution. We ask that you be mindful of the fact that we are here to *learn*."

The session chair introduced the three main speakers: Trimbach and his son John; Paul De-Main, editor of *News from Indian Country*, a print and electronic biweekly paper published in Wisconsin; and Denise Maloney, the daughter of Anna Mae Aquash, who would be tele-conferenced into the session. DeMain, fifty-five, was a member of the Oneida Nation of Wisconsin and had been writing about AIM misdeeds since 1994. He was unabashedly aligned with the anti-AIM crowd and volunteered to run Trimbach's PowerPoint presentation.

The bespectacled John Trimbach stood in front of the screen. He was a commercial airline pilot and air force veteran who looked like he was more than familiar with weight rooms. In 2008 father and son had self-published *American Indian Mafia*, a book that purported to expose AIM leaders as little more than a criminal gang. By the time it appeared, one low-ranking AIM member was already in prison for murdering Aquash, and another was about to stand trial.

John Trimbach

The Trimbachs and DeMain were convinced that the order to execute Aquash had come from high up.

Means, who took a seat in a back row with his wife, Pearl, would remain silent throughout the Trimbachs' presentation and would eventually leave in the middle of it, leaving Bellecourt and Paro to stick up for the movement.

"Folks, what I am about to share with you is troubling. But it is also documented, so please bear with me as we move along," John Trimbach began. "Listen to what I have to say and then make up your own minds. Let me begin by making a promise. We promise we won't lie to you. And you would expect that, but the reason I say that is because there are other speakers here who can't make the same claim because they have a vested interest in keeping you in the dark.

"You see, there are really two histories about Wounded Knee in '73. There is the history you're supposed to believe—what I call opiate for the masses: a story of how eighth-grade [-educated] Indians held up the mighty power of the U.S. government during seventy-two days of very public gunfire. And then there is the history of what really happened inside Wounded Knee, the history you're not supposed to know. You're not supposed to know that people were abducted and interrogated at Wounded Knee. You're not supposed to know that people were beaten and tortured at Wounded Knee. You're not supposed to know that people were raped and murdered at Wounded Knee. All of it behind barriers, and all of it instigated or condoned by the AIM leaders. People like Dennis Banks, Russell Means, Leonard Crow Dog, Carter Camp, Stan Holder." One by one, as John Trimbach spoke, DeMain flashed the former AIM leaders' pictures on the screen.

As the occupation wore on, Trimbach said, Banks became increasingly paranoid about spies in his midst. Holder, Camp, and Crow Dog, among others, had chained people to a bed and otherwise confined and interrogated them. "Some of the people who didn't pass the test ended up dead. We estimate that half a dozen people were murdered inside the village versus the one casualty who died from a stray government bullet."

The casualty Trimbach referred to was Buddy Lamont. Trimbach made no concession that Lamont's death, nor that of Frank Clear/Clearwater, had been caused by the government. Although the FBI and U.S. marshals, with the assistance and advice of the U.S. military, had pumped 500,000 rounds into the occupied village over the course of seventy-one days, the bullet that had killed Lamont was "stray." In fact, Trimbach alleged, Banks allowed Lamont to bleed to death as he lay in no-man's-land. Trimbach did not mention the names of the other six victims he said had been murdered inside the village, save one, Ray Robinson.

A picture of a lanky, smiling African-American man, sitting at what looked like a conference, flashed on the screen, followed by a picture of Robinson with his wife and children. It was ironic that representatives of the 1970s FBI were now championing his cause, for Robinson embodied everything the Hoover-led agency sought to crush in the 1960s. Carter Camp once told journalist Steven Hendricks, author of *The Unquiet Grave: The FBI and the Struggle for the Soul of Indian Country*, that Robinson had left the village on his own volition, that either he was turned over to Justice Department mediators or fell into the hands of Wilson's Goons, who had roughed up many of the "hippie" types they caught trying to sneak into the village. Wilson himself, in press conferences, threatened outsiders who supported the occupation.

That sounded plausible. But John Trimbach insisted that Robinson never left the village alive. He died in the infirmary, he said, and his body was buried nearby. Anna Mae Aquash was murdered, he asserted, because she knew about Robinson; and Dennis Banks's right-hand man, Leonard Peltier, had murdered FBI agents Coler and Williams near the Pine Ridge town of Oglala in 1975. The night before Aquash was executed, a dozen or so AIM members were at the home of Russell Means's brother Bill, where Aquash was brought against her will. There the decision was made to kill her, the Trimbachs and others allege.

In his presentation, Trimbach asserted that approximately twenty people were involved in the Aquash murder and the ensuing cover-up. At least six of them were Means's family members, plus Charles Abourezk. Trimbach quoted testimony given by Arlo Looking Cloud at a trial: "Charles Abourezk, the son of former senator James Abourezk, was at [Bill Means's] house the night they brought Anna Mae there before the others took her out and shot her in the head." Charles, a Rapid City attorney, was at the time, and remains to this day, an ardent AIM supporter.

Bill Means has denied in the press that Aquash was ever at his home.

Sometimes Trimbach judiciously used the word "allegedly" when accusing Dennis Banks of ordering Aquash's execution; other times he point-blank said he did it: "Banks was undoubtedly involved in the murder of Anna Mae. I believe he was behind the murder of Ray Robinson and many other victims at Wounded Knee, including Buddy Lamont," Trimbach said. He claimed that the government had called for a cease-fire and that Banks had left Lamont to lie in the open, bleeding, for two hours before agreeing.

Trimbach's half-hour presentation took on not only AIM but also left-wing academics who supported the movement and PBS for presenting a slanted documentary, *We Shall Remain*, which had interviewed his father but taken his quotes out of context. He ripped PBS affiliates for airing a documentary, *A Tattoo on My Heart: The Warriors of Wounded Knee 1973*, co-written and co-directed by Charles Abourezk. Authors such as Hendricks and Peter Matthiessen, who had written about FBI misconduct in the 1970s; newspapers for declining to review *American Indian Mafia*; the American Indian Museum in Washington, D.C., for refusing to stock the book; and the media in general—all were called dupes.

"The corruption in today's media has its roots in Wounded Knee," Trimbach declared, "the first large-scale historical event where the media abetted the criminals. . . . And the cover-up continues. What they don't understand is that when you promote liars, thieves, and killers as worthy role models and heroes of Indian Country, you do a huge disservice to Native Americans everywhere. These very opinionated academics and their friends in the media, they just don't get it. And so our book is ridiculed, ignored, or simply disposed of.

"There is a lot more I can tell, but we're running out of time. . . . Perhaps now you will understand why we call *American Indian Mafia* the history book they really don't want you to read."

From stage left, former Senator James Abourezk emerged from the standing-room-only crowd. He was now eighty-one years old but looking more

Former Senator James Abourezk

spry than his years. "I have a few questions, if I might," he said. "I wish my son were here. My son Charlie."

"I do too," John Trimbach replied.

"To hear you defame him like you defamed him. What you said was not a lie, but a goddam lie. . . ."

"I can see why you would feel that way," John said. The crowd applauded, but it wasn't clear who they were supporting.

"Just a minute. Just a minute," Abourezk said.

"Do you have a question, senator?"

"Let me finish. Do you want to let me finish, or do you want to talk some more?"

"No, finish the question."

"They had a federal criminal trial on Anna Mae Aquash up in Rapid City, and his name was mentioned by one of the witnesses as being there. And that was proved to be a goddam lie. . . ."

"No, it was not."

"Well, I'm sorry, it was."

"Well, I'm sorry, it wasn't."

"Then why isn't Charlie in jail right now? Tell me!"

"We'll get to him."

"You're going to do it, huh?"

"Hey, I'm not a prosecutor. All I'm trying to do is find—"

"Yes, you are a prosecutor. You sure sound like one."

"Well, so do you."

After this exchange, Abourezk recounted the story of how he and McGovern had traveled to Wounded Knee on the day following the take-over and negotiated the end of the occupation. Speaking directly to the elder Trimbach, who remained seated in the front row, leaning on his cane, Abourezk said, "And I went out and told you. Do you remember that?"

"I don't specifically remember . . ."

"That's what happened. I went back the next day to Washington thinking it was all over with, and it went on for *seventy more days*. Maybe you can tell me what happened that that deal fell apart. They were ready to give it up."

"Well," said Joe Trimbach, "they continued to fire at my agents and at the marshals. The agents merely defended themselves. There were several cease-fires, but then they broke the cease-fire. My agents didn't want to be there. They had no reason to want to go on. They wanted to go back home. . . . They didn't prolong it."

"Well, somebody prolonged it, because they were ready to give it up."

"It's all in our book, senator," John Trimbach interjected. "Read our book."

"I wouldn't spend a *nickel* on your book, sir!"

For years Paul DeMain and Clyde Bellecourt had tussled publicly over AIM's legacy. DeMain's interest dated from 1994, when he attended an AIM press conference held by Clyde's brother Vernon in St. Paul, about the Aquash and Peltier cases. The Bellecourts were firing salvos back at Means loyalists who were accusing them of involvement in Aquash's murder. When someone asked why the mainstream media were ignoring these cases, Vern pointed his finger at the Native American journalists sitting in the front row. If these Indian reporters weren't bothering to investigate these cases, why would anyone expect the non-Native media to care? he asked. DeMain took that as a personal challenge. He put together a team of Native journalists that included Harlan McKosato and Minnie Two Shoes, and they began conducting eyewitness interviews and digging into the thousands of documents available to them in various archives. At that time, like many young people who grew up in Indian communities, DeMain looked up to AIM leaders like the Bellecourts, Means, and Banks, and believed that Peltier had been wrongly convicted of murdering the two FBI agents. After sifting

American Indian Movement co-founder
Clyde Bellecourt

through all the evidence, DeMain became a crusading journalist—but not the kind that Vern had hoped. In fact DeMain was convinced that the leaders were culpable in several murders, including those of Aquash and Robinson. In an editorial in his newspaper, he declared that he believed Peltier was guilty.

As soon as DeMain stepped to the podium, Bellecourt began hectoring him. DeMain tried to power through his presentation. "As a journalist and writer, it's not that I don't think Clyde doesn't have the right to say what he has to say, or that he has a document that justifies a point that he made. . . . There are three thousand stories from people who were at Wounded Knee, Clyde. All their stories are legitimate. All of them are part of the elephant that we all are touching. As much as you may not agree with it, let us have our say."

DeMain began by making his case that Perry Ray Robinson had never left the occupied village. John Trimbach passed around transcripts of interviews DeMain had conducted over the years as well as a picture of Robinson. "The issue of a black man being buried at Wounded Knee I think is pretty well confirmed by participants who were there," DeMain said. He mentioned other allegations and rumors that had arisen over the years—of women who were killed and raped by Goons and their bodies buried in the hills; of a "Sicilian," mentioned in one interview by Leonard Crow Dog, who was allegedly killed and buried there; of six victims who, according to the Trimbachs, were killed and secretly buried there. (Unlike the Robinson case, no family members of other purported victims have come forward, nor have the Trimbachs or DeMain produced the victims' names.)

All along, Bellecourt continued to interrupt with a steady stream of accusations, bringing up the fact that DeMain's ex-wife was in prison for embezzlement, calling him a liar, and so on.

DeMain said it was up to the residents of Pine Ridge to finally put an end to the AIM charades. Since only premeditated murder could be prosecuted after so many years, it was unlikely that any of the other crimes would go to court. Based on the evidence of eyewitness accounts, he didn't think there would be a first-degree murder charge in Robinson's case.

"It is really time to bring people together and resolve what happened on Pine Ridge," DeMain concluded. "I like Clyde. There are things I respect about him. . . . You got stories to tell that are good, bad, and ugly, don't you? We all do, we all do. You got people who want to tell the truth. You got people like Clyde who want to stand up and try to intimidate us. . . . They have their own media. They have written their own books. I looked up to them for a long time as courageous people, but he is a liar. . . . I would really ask on behalf of the people who were buried in Wounded Knee, South Dakota, from 1973: help bring them back home. If it is a forum where people are forgiven and given immunity or something, let's get this charade over. Help bring Perry Ray Robinson home. Let's bring the Sicilian guy Leonard Crow Dog talks about being buried down there and some other people if they are there. Let's help bring them home in a good way. So we can get on with all of the good legacy that you guys did without this garbage."

Denise Maloney, the eldest daughter of Anna-Mae Pictou-Aquash, speaking through a computer feed from Nova Scotia, Canada, began her recollections by insisting that she too was not an FBI dupe. "Please do not confuse the fact that I am sharing a time spot and a stage with John Trimbach as an opportunity to again prove that I am in with the feds," she said.

The last time Denise had seen her mother alive was in the fall of 1975 before her captivity, when Anna Mae sneaked into Canada to visit her girls, who were living with her first husband. She told them she had to go back to clear her name, and that she was fighting for their future and the future of all Native Americans. She would call them at Christmas, she promised. Aquash had spent time as Banks's lover, though he was married to a young Lakota woman, and Aquash truly believed in AIM's cause. Apparently she could not extricate herself from the movement and returned to the United States.

By December 1975, Aquash had been held against her will in a series of Denver, Rapid City, and reservation safe houses, including that of Bill Means, where several other AIM members had seen her. The movement had become convinced she was an FBI informant. She had been questioned by the FBI once and arrested twice but released on bond. AIM members wondered why the FBI would let her go so many times when she was wanted on weapons charges. Before her visit to Canada, Peltier had interrogated her at gunpoint. She knew she was under suspicion, but she could not leave the movement.

Peltier's paranoia was well founded. He was present when FBI agents Ron Williams and Jack Coler came barreling in their unmarked cars into an AIM stronghold on Pine Ridge, near the town of Oglala on June 26, 1975. AIM members exchanged fire with the two men, who were soon overwhelmed, surrounded and injured. Peltier would eventually be convicted of shooting the two incapacitated men at close range.

The question among AIM leaders was what to do about Aquash. The stakes were high, because leaks could hang the Coler and Williams murders on Peltier.

During her captivity Aquash had been beaten and raped. After she was allegedly taken to Bill Means's home, three rank-and-file AIM members, Arlo Looking Cloud, John Boy Graham, and Theda Nelson Clark, took Aquash to the edge of a cliff on the remote northeast corner of the Pine Ridge Reservation. As Clark stayed in her red Ford Pinto and watched, Graham shot her in the back of the head, and the pair dumped the body into a ravine, where it went undiscovered until February 1976.

For decades Aquash's death was a notorious unsolved mystery on the reservation. After two trials in the 2000s, Looking Cloud and Graham were convicted of the crime and are now serving life terms. Thelma Rios, who pleaded guilty to opening her apartment to allow Aquash to be held and interrogated there, received a suspended sentence, then died of lung cancer shortly thereafter. Richard Marshall, who was accused of supplying the handgun, was acquitted. Theda Nelson Clark, said to be incompetent to stand trial and living in a nursing home, was never charged.

Maloney, the Trimbachs, and DeMain are all convinced that Vern Bellecourt, after conferring with Clyde in a phone call, ordered the execution. Banks, they allege, knew about the crime after the fact and was complicit in covering it up. But none of those convicted have ever fingered the Bellecourts as ordering them to kill Aquash. DeMain has become a confidant of Looking Cloud, who has told him that he was angry at the Minneapolis-based leaders, but he has never directly told him why, or expressly said that he received orders from higher up.

Maloney spoke through the thin internet connection: "When you are discussing the taking of another human being's life, there is no debate. There is no side to take in kidnapping someone. There is no side to take in doing an interrogation. There is no side to take in the murder and rape of a human being. There is no side to take in pointing and putting a bullet in the back of a skull. And there certainly is no side to take when dumping another human being's remains in the side of a ditch like a bag of garbage. It is wrong. Plain and simple."

In the years following her death, AIM leaders never contacted the Aquash family to see how they were doing, Maloney said. "I want to know why AIM leadership never investigated the murder of Anna Mae. I want to know why they never contacted our family in thirty-six years. I want to know why they refuse to address her murder to this day. I want to know why they lied and continue to lie that it was the FBI that murdered Anna Mae."

The moderator asked if there were any questions. Bellecourt, who had never ceased to comment during the earlier presentations, now sat quietly, his lips clenched in a frown. He, Banks, and Means would refuse to comment on Aquash's murder for the remainder of the conference.

Cheryl Buswell-Robinson, Ray's widow, was given a few minutes to speak. At John Trimbach's expense she had flown to the conference from Detroit, where she remained active in liberal causes. A short white woman with thick glasses, now sixty-seven, she wanted to tell the audience, first, that her husband was not an FBI informant, as had been rumored. "Informers *don't act like that*. They don't have the *commitment* that my husband had. So I don't want to hear any smear

Cheryl Buswell-Robinson

of my husband, ever because—." She stopped to collect herself and wipe away a tear. "—His life was the movement. The movement came before me. The movement came before his kids. The last time I spoke with him, he said, 'Come with me to Wounded Knee,' because they had sent a speaker to a conference he was at and said they needed reinforcements. 'This is the spark that will start a prairie fire.' I said, 'No, it's not.' I argued with him. I begged him. I pleaded with him. Please come back. We were growing food for the Black Panther party in Alabama, outside Selma. It was time for spring planting.

"'No,' he said. 'Bring the kids, we'll go inside Wounded Knee together.'

"'No, we won't.'

"That was the last time I talked to him. We were arguing. I regret it to this day." She talked as the tears welled up again. "All I ask is to have his body. Let me know so that I can take him home and he can have a proper burial."

The question-and-answer period began with sharp exchanges between Joe Trimbach and Bellecourt over the trial of Banks and Means that took place in St. Paul the year after the occupation. Bellecourt then stood up and asserted that the Wounded Knee occupation had been intended as peaceful. "There is something I want to correct before we go on much further. When we went into Wounded Knee it was to be a peaceful occupation, so that we could bring people like Senator James Abourezk and McGovern and others to come there and make some kind of commitment. . . . We asked all the residents and the women to leave because they said they were going to come in by five o'clock and wipe us out." Not one resident wanted to leave, Bellecourt said.

A journalist asked Joe Trimbach how many informants were inside the village. "I don't honestly know," he replied, "because I was only there two weeks. After that I was totally removed from the case." (*American Indian Mafia* notes four informants inside the village during Trimbach's time there: one special agent who was undercover, an unnamed "source," and two journalists who described to the FBI what they had seen.)

Adrienne Fritze, for the first time during the conference, stood up to speak. For decades she had carried the bitterness of what had happened to her and her family. She and her eighty-six-year-old mother Jeanne were the last of the dozen hostages taken by AIM who were still alive. She took exception to Bellecourt's comments about peaceful intentions.

Fritze had come to the conference from Seattle, also with some airfare help from John

Trimbach, under the mistaken belief that the event was dedicated to reconciliation. In fact, none of the literature or preconference publicity had claimed that it was anything other than an academic history conference. Still, Adrienne had come for some kind of closure. This was the first time in nearly four decades that she had the opportunity to look the perpetrators in the eye.

"I was there," she said. "I was twelve years old. You came in. You and other militants and supporters. You shot out the lights, the streetlights. You broke into the museum."

"You have been scripted by Paul DeMain," Bellecourt responded.

"There were guns in the trading post. They came in the front door, the back door, broke them down. My grandfather was a paraplegic. He spent his entire life collecting artifacts and the stories of the Lakota people whom he grew to love, even though we were Ojibwe. . . . I can't even begin to tell you the terror I felt as a twelve-year-old. We were bullied and pushed around and threatened by adults. . . . I can't believe you have the gall to say that I am lying."

"I never fought with anybody at Wounded Knee. I never carried a gun," Bellecourt replied. He insisted that all the hostages were well cared for.

Fritze reminded him that they were distant cousins. It was a point that needed to be made. The fact that Agnes Gildersleeve was part Indian, as was her brother Wilbur and her sister Mary, had been whitewashed from most AIM-sympathetic history books.

Both Banks and Means asserted in their autobiographies that the armed guards were there to protect the Gildersleeves from the angry local residents, who despised them for their corrupt business practices. AIM has continued to insist that the residents of Wounded Knee were free to go but preferred to stay. Yet there is plenty of documented evidence indicating that the AIM leaders initially considered them hostages and bargaining chips.

"I am shaking so much it is unbelievable," Adrienne continued. "The brutality happened. You guys perpetrated it. Some of us believed that you could bring freedom, but you took it away from us."

RUSSELL MEANS RESPONDS

Of all the speakers who came to Sioux Falls that day, only Russell Means could pack a room the size of the Chapel of Reconciliation. Two hundred seventy-five people had paid ten dollars each for an opportunity to hear him talk on Friday evening. The audience filed in and took their seats on the hard wooden pews, some coming from a sold-out dinner nearby where they had heard a relatively unknown author speak about AIM's early years. Others came to the campus

Former AIM leader Russell Means

especially to hear Means. A large group of Native American teenagers were among the last to take their seats. The chapel had three sections, one on either side of the pulpit and one directly facing it. Means, his wife, Pearl, and Ward Churchill settled in the front row, stage right, and Clyde Bellecourt sat alone about as far away as he could on the opposite side. Neither seemed to want to be close enough to share the same air.

That evening the Chapel of Reconciliation may have been an ironic locale—there had been little resolution during the heated arguments of the afternoon—but suddenly it promised to live up to its name. A few minutes before the lecture was about to begin, Bellecourt rose to his feet and walked over to shake Means's hand. They shared a few words, and Bellecourt returned to his seat.

Harry Thompson began the introduction by starting with a quote found in Means's own publicity. "The *Los Angeles Times* called him the most famous Indian since Sitting Bull and Crazy Horse." Then he went outside the official biography to read from an October 2011 column written by longtime Oglala journalist and newspaper publisher Tim Giago, who had often been a strident AIM critic through the years. The column had appeared when it was widely believed that cancer would soon take Means's life.

"Like the enigma he was, Means often went from the practical to the ridiculous, but he always had the courage of his convictions. He sincerely believed that it was his goal in life to crush the bureaucracy that covertly impoverished and attempted to annihilate the cultures of his people," Thompson read. And he introduced the speaker.

Means walked to the pulpit to vigorous applause that lasted nearly a minute. He wore a pair of large bifocals, took a swig from his blue-and-white water bottle, and began a one-hour-and-twenty-two-minute speech in defense of AIM. He had no notes, of course. He never did. Means could speak extemporaneously for hours if he chose. He did not have the vigor that he possessed before his illness—there was a slight slur in his speech—but he could still deliver a punch line to end an anecdote. In his prime his fiery speeches were something to behold. But he was no longer in his prime.

After speaking of his childhood and memories of his parents, Means turned to his early involvement in AIM. Banks and Bellecourt had invited him to join them at a National Council of Churches meeting in Detroit. For years the Council had been handing out literature portraying bedraggled and malnourished Indian children, and asking parishioners for donations. Yet almost none of that money was making its way to Native children, AIM believed. Bellecourt went to the microphone at the conference and launched a harangue that wouldn't end.

"Clyde likes to talk. And he knows his Christian history. They accepted the challenges," Means said as Bellecourt laughed and nodded from his seat in the pews.

Means was impressed enough to join AIM, quit his job as an accountant in Cleveland, and give his life over to the movement. That was 1969, and for the next twenty-five years the money donated to the National Council of Churches program was controlled by a board of directors comprising Native American clergy. "Millions of dollars went to Christian Indians because of AIM. Christian Indians and their denominations' programs. To this day we have never received a thank you," Means said.

In the Minneapolis Indian neighborhoods, Means recalled, AIM reduced police brutality by organizing street patrols that quelled disturbances before the cops arrived. They successfully forced the Minnesota school board to change the unbalanced history books that portrayed Indians as savages.

"At the time we organized in twenty different cities, there were over two dozen Indian organizations—all of them social clubs, none of them an advocate for Indian rights. . . . The beginnings of my experience with AIM and those things are never talked about. I never saw any violence except on the part of the police.

"I saw them accomplish goal after goal after goal. AIM was in a lot of respects ahead of itself." But this was a different kind of movement. Its axiom was: "We don't turn the other cheek, nor do we bend over and give the other to you to kick. You hit us, we are coming after you."

After this preamble, Means arrived at the accusations the Trimbachs had hurled at AIM earlier that day. He held up a thick document produced by the Senate Select Committee to Study Governmental Operations with Respect to Intelligence Activities, better known as the Church Committee (after Frank Church, the Idaho senator). The post-Watergate years were a time for left-leaning lawmakers to fire back at the administration. FBI chief Hoover was dead, mistrust of government was at an all-time high, and the Church Committee began looking under rocks. The FBI came under scrutiny for its counterintelligence program COINTELPRO, which had been directed at 1960s dissidents, white supremacists, and civil rights activists.

Means plopped a stack of Church Committee documents on the podium along with transcripts from the eight-month Wounded Knee leadership trial that took place in St. Paul. "What the FBI did. It's all in here. It's all in here! . . . Example after example after example of how the FBI fabricated evidence, withheld evidence, and altered evidence. All three. They put known liars on the stand!"

He continued: "Trimbach was one of the biggest violators . . . and it's all in the transcripts. I was going to read it to you, but by the time I got through reading it, there would be nobody here."

Means bragged that AIM had destroyed the Bureau of Indian Affairs during the occupation of its Washington headquarters in 1972 and had smuggled out tons of documents. The muckraking columnist Jack Anderson drew on them afterward in a series of columns that exposed the bureau's corruption and ineptitude. "No one ever remembers that. The [columns] lasted for months and months. No one ever went to prison. The Bureau of Indian Affairs was out of service for six weeks. And nobody missed them. Nobody missed them. Not a complaint!" he said, as the audience chuckled.

"The persona of AIM and violence are almost synonymous. And all we did was refuse to turn the other cheek and bend over and give the other to kick. You weren't going to kick around American Indians anymore," he said, becoming more emotional. "That wasn't going to happen! No more relocation! No more stealing our land! No more damning up our rivers and stealing our land!"

The audience applauded vigorously.

"And guess what else happened. We were the catalyst to get rid of the boarding-school system, the religious boarding schools and the government boarding schools where they tortured and killed our kids. . . . I didn't find out until my mother was deceased that she was raped, right down here at the St. Mary's Episcopal School for Girls. And it's a damn good thing I found out after she was deceased and in the next world.

"You don't have a clue about the cruelty. . . . We couldn't speak our languages without physical torture. I would like some of you people to sit there with your parents and hear some of the atrocities. That's what we grew up with: FEAR! FEAR! You don't have a clue."

In the midst of Means's remarks, thunder cracked and rumbled outside. "That's a good sign. That's a good sign. Holy! That says something

good. The thunder spirits are here!" For the remainder of the talk, rain pounded steadily on the
roof.

"You are continuing to allow the government
to violate the Constitution of the United States of
America on a daily basis with us," Means told his
audience. "It's come to you, hasn't it? Now your
representatives are corrupt. The Supreme Court
is political instead of judicial. Your president is
a quasi-king. It gets worse and worse. The illegal, outlaw FBI is now the Secret Service for the
United States government. You have lost all your
individual rights. You're the new Indians! You're
the new Indians! Welcome aboard!"

Finally Means thanked the organizers and
entertained questions. The first came from a
young white man who went to the microphone
to ask about Leonard Peltier. He expressed surprise that Means hadn't mentioned him. Indeed,
he had said almost nothing about the Wounded
Knee occupation and nary a word about its ugly
aftermath: the execution of Anna Mae Aquash
and the cold-blooded murder of FBI agents Coler
and Williams by an AIM member or members.
Or the subsequent conviction of Peltier, who
many in the Native American community believe was wrongly sentenced to two consecutive
life terms.

"I'm kind of curious that through all this I did not hear the name Leonard Peltier," the young man said, apparently not knowing much about AIM's history and the schism between Means and Banks that existed during the time of the incident. Peltier had been a confidant of Banks.

"What about Leonard Peltier?" Means replied somewhat defensively, not knowing that this was a sympathetic question.

"Was he a friend of yours? Was he involved in Wounded Knee as well?"

"Leonard was never in Wounded Knee. He was over at Leonard Crow Dog's place. No, he never came to Wounded Knee."

"Well, do you think he is imprisoned falsely?"

"Oh, he is going to die in prison."

"You think so?"

"He is the prime example of anti-Indian sentiment in this country. They don't care. Any Indian will do," Means replied, deftly dodging the real question.

"Well, I agree with you 100 percent," said the man. "I thought we had a president at one time that might free him. I was disappointed it didn't happen. But I think we may have one in office right now that will do that. I was wondering if you have ever had an audience with the president over this situation. Have you?"

"No, I haven't."

Means received a standing ovation. His contractual obligation with the college was finished, but he wasn't leaving Sioux Falls that night. He would stay for the following day's panels and lunch. Reinforcements in the fight over AIM's legacy were on the way.

UNITED STATES VS. BANKS AND MEANS

The occupation at Wounded Knee lasted almost two and a half months; the trial of Dennis Banks and Russell Means that opened in St. Paul on January 8, 1974, on a bevy of charges stemming from the occupation, would last eight. Judge Fred Nichol moved the proceedings to Minnesota because the defense attorneys had made a compelling case that the defendants could not receive a fair trial in South Dakota, where anti-AIM sentiment was running high.

Nichol had been appointed to the U.S. District Court for the District of South Dakota by President Johnson in 1965 and was a close friend of Senator McGovern. Like many federal judges who depended on presidential appointments to secure their jobs, he swung a certain political way, and he was firmly in the Democrats' camp. Nichol presided over the controversial trial just as the Nixon administration was sinking. The Watergate break-ins were catching up with the Republican president. Some of the accusations hurled at his administration—illegal wiretapping, for example—would have echoes in the trial about Wounded Knee.

When it came to civil liberties, the legal profession, like the nation itself, had split into warring camps. Many lawyers on the right were convinced that protest and the investigative reporting of establishment misdeeds had gone too far. But the attorneys who became celebrities were those who had cut their teeth defending civil rights activists in the 1960s. As the occupation at Wounded Knee dragged on, they were already gathering forces, donating their time, and raising funds for the anticipated legal battles ahead. And as the trial approached, an army of lawyers, many from the left-leaning National Lawyers Guild, set up offices in Rapid City, South Dakota, to plan the AIM leaders' defense. Some of these attorneys were young idealists, fresh out of law school, who volunteered for a few weeks or months. Others were highly experienced and had earlier run up against the might of the federal government and the FBI. Meanwhile AIM representatives spread out across the nation and even in Western Europe to raise funds.

Leading the defense was one of the best-known lawyers in America, William Kunstler. Fifty-five years old at the time of the trial, Kunstler had earned his fame by defending the Chicago Seven for conspiring to incite a riot at the 1968 Democratic National Convention in Chicago. He had exposed FBI wrongdoings in that case and was prepared to do the same in this one. A relentless self-promoter, he relished his role as a "radical lawyer."

Mark Lane, forty-seven, who had spent his career fighting for civil rights and trade unions, and had gone up against Senator Joe McCarthy's subcommittee, also joined the team. Lane was perhaps best known for his book *Rush to Judgment*, which sought to debunk the Warren Report on the Kennedy assassination. Ken Tilsen, also forty-seven, while not as famous as Kunstler and Lane, had defended draft dodgers and black civil rights activists in the 1960s and was a St. Paul native. Tilsen coordinated the Wounded Knee Legal Defense and Offense Committee, WKLDOC, which AIM had formed with the attorneys.

Bellecourt's accusations at the 2012 conference may have come across as a left-wing conspiracy theory rant, but there was no denying that the FBI and the prosecutors made numerous and egregious mistakes that resulted in an ignoble dismissal of all charges. The portrait of Judge Nichol that was painted by the Trimbachs as a Nixon-hating Democrat probably had more than a few grains of truth. But during their presentation, John Trimbach had glossed over the fodder that the FBI and his father had provided the judge, which allowed him to dismiss the case for perfectly legitimate reasons.

John Trimbach described the trial as a "circus." But if that were the case, Joe Trimbach and the FBI stood squarely in one of Barnum & Bailey's three rings. Judge Nichol, who made little effort to hide his contempt for the FBI, occupied the second, and the defendants and their bombastic, media-savvy attorneys were in the third.

Indeed, the trial at times degenerated into a spectacle. It began with Nichol granting the highly unusual request to allow Banks and Means to serve as co-counsel on the legal team. They could therefore be allowed to give opening statements to the jury without later having to testify and be cross-examined about their content. The defendants and the legal team let it be known to the press and through the opening remarks that this would not be a trial over a series of crimes committed during the occupation. It would be an indictment against the U.S. government and its nearly two hundred years of mistreatment of Native Americans, the Lakotas in particular. They would ask Nichol to rule that the Treaty of 1868, designed to "ensure the civilization" of the Lakotas, was still in force and therefore that the FBI and the courts had no jurisdiction over crimes committed by Indians on Indian lands.

U.S. Assistant Attorney Richard D. Hurd led the prosecution team with David Gienapp serving as co-counsel. Both were thirty-two years old, South Dakota–born and –bred. A junior Justice Department attorney was there to aid them, and one senior to them was occasionally on hand to offer advice; but this was their show. They wanted the defendants put away for crimes that took place during the armed insurrection. But they were up against a vastly more experienced six-member defense team, which had a small army of volunteers available to track down and research every fact the prosecution presented. Hurd had the FBI as his investigative arm, but at times he probably wished he hadn't.

One of the first controversies to erupt in the trial concerned a wiretap placed on the sole phone line leading into the village. Lane had been tipped off by a phone company employee that he had installed a party line that led to one of the government roadblocks. The defense alleged that this line was used illegally to monitor confidential attorney-client conversations. Trimbach, faced with this accusation, testified in the judge's chambers on two occasions that he had never authorized or sought a wiretap.

That proved to be wrong. Suspecting that documents confirming their allegation existed, and had not been turned over to the defense as ordered, Kunstler and Lane demanded that the FBI again comb its records for any such request. Eventually the bureau handed over an incomplete one-page document that did in fact request a wiretap on the phone line. Two pages were missing. Getting those pages to be entered into evidence was like pulling teeth—but it turned out that they had Trimbach's signature. FBI agents' reports of conversations they had listened in on had been forwarded to Trimbach, who put his initials on those as well. And then a second wiretap application surfaced later in the hearing.

Trimbach was brought before the judge, who warned him about self-incrimination and his Fifth Amendment rights before questioning him about the evidence. With a possible perjury charge hanging over his head, Trimbach maintained that the occupation was a tiring time, that he had been functioning with little sleep, and that he must have forgotten he signed the order.

The story on the wiretap seemed to change each day of the trial as a long line of FBI agents and marshals came forward to testify about listening in on the party line that Trimbach initially said didn't exist. Some said it was used simply to arrange negotiations—though the Justice Department's lead negotiator testified that he knew nothing about it. Others said it was needed to gather intelligence on booby traps that could endanger lives.

Other circumstantial evidence revealed that the FBI had purchased ninety cassette tapes and that the marshals had been given unfettered access to the Pine Ridge telephone building, where eavesdropping could have occurred. An FBI team that specialized in eavesdropping arrived on Pine Ridge with wiretapping equipment, in anticipation of an approval that never legally came. But they didn't leave until April.

Nichol was visibly angry at these revelations and could have dismissed the government's case then, but he said he would let the trial proceed in the interest of justice. He warned Hurd and Gienapp that he would dismiss the case if there were any other shenanigans by the government. It had taken five weeks of testimony to get to the bottom of the wiretap, all outside the presence of the jury. Five weeks of jury selection, five weeks of the wiretap controversy, and the circus still wasn't truly under way.

Other trial developments made headlines. Numerous times the defense, particularly Kunstler, drew Nichol's ire. In all his years as a self-proclaimed "radical lawyer," Kunstler had never spent a night in jail on contempt-of-court charges. But he did in St. Paul after launching a rant against the judge, who had asked marshals to clear out a row of AIM supporters in the court-room because of their laughing. Lane too would spend a night in jail for contempt for failing to heed Nichol's order to stop badgering a prosecu-tion witness.

Several notable performers were on hand for the trial. When Marlon Brando, an ardent sup-porter of AIM and Native American rights in general, came to St. Paul to lend his voice, lo-cal reporters gathered around for quotes on the courthouse steps. One of the witnesses for the prosecution was FBI Acting Associate Director Mark Felt, who decades later would be revealed as the Deep Throat who helped *Washington Post* reporters Bob Woodward and Carl Bernstein uncover the Watergate scandal.

One FBI agent who testified that he had lis-tened in on phone conversations coming from the Wounded Knee trading post was chased out of the courthouse by Banks and other AIM members who threatened to place him under cit-izen's arrest. Marshals had to whisk him away. In another odd incident, a pair of FBI agents were caught standing behind a courtroom side door listening in on the proceedings. Kunstler noticed the side door continuously cracking open, then closing. When he walked up and yanked it open, the two agents stumbled into the courtroom.

There was no doubt that AIM members had exchanged gunfire with federal officers, made Molotov cocktails, and looted the general store, but the evidence that Banks and Means themselves had carried out such actions was scant. The Gildersleeves and the Fritzes, including Adrienne, took the stand to testify to the destruction in the village. The prosecution trotted out the marshals and FBI agents who had been wounded during the firefights. But other than one decidedly pro-Wilson witness, little evidence connected Banks and Means directly to any of these acts. The only charge that might stick was conspiracy—if the prosecution could prove that the two leaders had given the orders to shoot.

Evidence was so scant that when it came time for the defense to present its case, it ignored the charges and instead brought in Vine Deloria, Jr., and Dee Brown, authors of *Custer Died for Your Sins* and *Bury My Heart at Wounded Knee*, respectively, as witnesses. They testified generally about treaty obligations and the mistreatment of Native Americans. Other Pine Ridge residents spoke about the reservation's deplorable conditions and the repression they experienced under tribal president Wilson.

As the trial wound down, Judge Nichol found that the military had violated the Posse Comitatus Act, which prevent the armed forces from interfering in civil matters without congressional authorization or the presidential declaration of a civil disorder. The defense presented evidence that equipment had been supplied and maintained by the military during the occupation, including fifteen armored personnel carriers, at a cost of $500,000, and that two high-ranking military advisers had been on hand. Judge Nichol therefore dismissed charges of obstruction of marshals and FBI agents "engaged in the lawful performance of their duties," declaring that they had not acted lawfully.

In an apparent act of desperation, the prosecution provided a surprise rebuttal witness: Louis Moves Camp, who along with his staunch AIM-supporting mother, Ellen Moves Camp, had been present in Wounded Knee. He was twenty-two years old and a Pine Ridge native who had recently run afoul of the law on a series of charges unrelated to the protest. Louis took the stand and declared that he had witnessed Banks and Means fire weapons at FBI positions, steal items from the trading post, and order others to take hostages and make Molotov cocktails. This prompted his mother to bolt out of the gallery and announce that her son was lying, that the FBI had made him fabricate the story. Judge Nichol was furious and initially accused Kunstler and the defense of orchestrating the scene.

Moves Camp's testimony appeared to be damaging. But in cross-examination Kunstler caught him in several lies and contradictions. Further, he revealed that Moves Camp had five federal charges pending against him at the time he approached the FBI about testifying. Most disturbing was an alleged rape that Moves Camp had committed while FBI agents, including David Price and his partner Ron Williams, had him under wraps in Wisconsin awaiting trial. Moves Camp had allegedly brought a local teenager back to his room after a night of barhopping. She later went to the local sheriff and filed a complaint. The defense believed that Price and the FBI had acted to suppress that case so Moves Camp could testify. This allegation was never proven, but it raised the question of whether Moves Camp had been making up stories in exchange for immunity, which the prosecution denied.

Most damaging, WKLDOC investigators discovered that Moves Camp had been fund-raising for AIM in California during many of the events he described—and had appeared on television shows and in front of large audiences. Hurd later told the court that he had asked Trimbach if they could give Moves Camp a lie detector test to confirm his story, but the FBI agent turned him down. It was Hurd's prerogative to demand one anyway, but he did not.

Eight months and more than 150 witnesses after the opening of the trial, the attorneys presented their closing statements. Judge Nichol gave the jury its instructions, and the six men and six women, all white, began their deliberations. Despite the Moves Camp charade, Nichol allowed the conspiracy charge to stand.

Hurd and Gienapp were undoubtedly pessimistic. Nichol was clearly angry that the prosecution and the FBI had not initially produced all the documents regarding the illegal wiretap, and had brought to the stand a witness who was spinning lies. In the course of the trial the judge made several references comparing the case to the unfolding Watergate scandal, which provided ammunition for his critics who claimed that hatred of Nixon was coloring his judgments. Nevertheless, despite claims four decades later at the 2012 conference that Nichol had been biased in favor of AIM, he sent theft and conspiracy counts to the jury, which took the verdict out of his hands.

As jury deliberations began, one of the jurors fell ill. Interviews with dismissed alternate jurors that now appeared in the press indicated that the jury was leaning toward the defendants. The deliberations could have continued with eleven jury members if both sides and the judge agreed, but Hurd and Gienapp, under orders from the Justice Department, objected. They hoped for a mistrial that would allow them to prosecute the case under more favorable circumstances—the most favorable being a new judge. But Hurd made the mistake of telling that to a reporter.

Acting swiftly, the defense presented to Nichol a document listing all the instances of government malfeasance during the trial, and asked for dismissal. At the 2012 conference, John Trimbach would call the action a secret conspiracy between the defense and Nichol, but it was done with Hurd present.

Nichol dismissed all charges, taking an hour to denounce Trimbach and Hurd for their conduct. He noted that the special agent in charge had claimed in court to have vetted Moves Camp and checked out his story, and then refused prosecution's attempts to give him a lie detector test. Hurd's admission that he wanted a mistrial in order to get a more favorable judge went against the letter of the law, Nichol said, and "violated the spirit in which a prosecutor should function." His duty was to seek justice, not a conviction.

"I'm rather ashamed that our government was not represented better in the trial of this case," Nichol added.

Ken Tilsen told the press that one of the prosecution's biggest mistakes was that it first filed charges, then went about trying to find evidence to back them up. And strong evidence that might have convicted Means and Banks never emerged in the trial.

Amazingly, an armed insurrection that involved the taking of hostages and the theft and destruction of personal property, in full view of TV cameras, with Banks and Means overtly leading the operation, failed to produce a conviction on any count. For the Justice Department and the FBI, this was a huge embarrassment. Not on the scale of Watergate, but a fiasco nonetheless. By the time the trial ended, Nixon had resigned. Mistrust of the government reached an all-time high, and the headlines coming out of St. Paul only added fuel to the fire.

✳   ✳   ✳

Session 15 of the conference at the Center for Western Studies, the panel on "Investigations and Prosecutions Arising out of the 1973 Wounded Knee Occupation," lacked a certain balance. David Gienapp, by then a third circuit

(From left to right) Judge David Gienapp; former Wounded Knee resident Adrienne Fritze; former prosecuting attorney James McMahon and former FBI Special Agent David Price

presiding judge for the state of South Dakota, was on hand along with David Price, the former FBI field agent who had served on Pine Ridge for four years, from the occupation to the killing of his colleagues Coler and Williams, the Aquash case, and dozens of other high-profile incidents. He was also one of the two agents who had kept Moves Camp at a Wisconsin dude ranch before the Banks-Means trial and testified that he had offered him nearly two thousand dollars in witness and relocation fees. But he had sworn under oath that he never tried to quash the state rape charges.

As South Dakota governor, Bill Janklow, one of AIM's most fervent enemies, had later appointed both prosecution attorneys as state judges. Hurd had died in 1995; Gienapp would announce his intention to retire from the bench by the end of 2012. Janklow had agreed to appear at the conference and would undoubtedly have been a keynote speaker, but he had died of brain cancer in January.

Also on the panel was James McMahon, a former prosecuting attorney who had brought Arlo Looking Cloud, one of Anna Mae Aquash's murderers, to justice. Perhaps a little out of place on the panel, by her own admission, was Adrienne Fritze. As a thirteen-year-old, she and almost all of her extended family who had lived in Wounded Knee, including Agnes Gildersleeve, had testified at the trial about the first harrowing days of the occupation.

Ken Tilsen, eighty-four at the time of the conference, was very much alive and kicking, and told the press that he felt snubbed that he hadn't been invited by the organizers. Noting that Trimbach and Gienapp were presenting, and he wasn't, he slammed *American Indian Mafia* and said the attendees would be getting a distorted account of the trial. Tilsen wrote to Thompson: "Will the conference be made aware of the documented misconduct of the FBI and the prosecution found to have taken place during the trial of Dennis Banks and Russell Means in St. Paul?" The answer would be "yes," but only through the efforts of Clyde Bellecourt, who during the FBI panel had to shout over Paul DeMain and John Trimbach.

Harry Thompson, the conference organizer, had a somewhat passive policy about participants. He had sent word about the conference far and wide, and those who were interested contacted him and proposed topics. Such was the case with the Trimbachs, who organized their own panel and were given a time slot of more than two hours. Thompson said Tilsen was not

"not invited," adding that he was free to come to the conference and participate. Indeed, some who were not on the schedule, such as Adrienne Fritze and Clyde Bellecourt, ended up with numerous opportunities to speak.

During the Q&A following the Trimbachs' contentious FBI panel the previous day, Joe had responded to questions about the wiretapping incident. It was all covered in the trial, he said, and there was nothing left to say about it. He stood by his testimony: he had simply forgotten that he had signed the document. If he had committed perjury, Judge Nichol would have charged him, he added.

During his presentation, John Trimbach had made several allegations about Nichol. "Before [the trial] even began," Trimbach said, "Judge Nichol invited Dennis Banks and his lawyer to his house where Banks made the judge's wife an honorary member of AIM. And nine months later, when the jury was finally allowed to deliberate, Judge Nichol called a secret *ex partie* meeting with [AIM attorneys] where together they drew up the dismissal order. Interesting side note: my father believes he had a mole in his office, or possibly Judge Nichol's office. I believe it was the judge himself. When he found out that FBI informant Douglas Durham was also in his house, the judge blew his top. That's when somebody blew Durham's cover."

If Durham had not been exposed, Trimbach told the audience, he could have warned Anna Mae Aquash that AIM leaders were planning to execute her.

"Some liberal do-gooder, perhaps Judge Nichol himself, helped Anna Mae get killed," Trimbach said.

One of the allegations that emerged during the trial was that the FBI had placed an informant inside the defense's legal team as it prepared for the trial. That may have turned out to be true when Douglas Durham was exposed. The Trimbachs' book claims that Durham was a low-level gopher and was never a party to defense strategies—which seemingly contradicts the assertion that he would have been close enough to the leadership to hear of a plan to execute Aquash.

Gienapp, nearing seventy years old, was now portly with a receding hairline. As part of the panel he described a barebones Justice Department operation in South Dakota when AIM asserted itself there. He was one of three assistant U.S. attorneys whose territory was the entire state, including major crimes on all the reservations, federal crimes outside the reservations, and routine noncriminal land condemnation cases.

Altogether Gienapp had tried forty cases in front of Nichol as a U.S. attorney and in private practice. "Except for one case, he was a wonderful judge. A wonderful individual to deal with," he said. The Leadership Trial, as he called it, "was an entirely different world. A litany of mistakes, errors, things that a judge should not do.

"The reason was," Gienapp continued, "Nichol was a very political individual. He was a stern Democrat, a very close friend of George McGovern, who got him his position. George McGovern got beat. He did not like Richard Nixon. The defense counsel, Lane and Kunstler, played Watergate and Nixon to the nth degree. They knew how to pluck those strings and did a very good job of plucking those strings."

The only government agency around as a target for Nichol's anger was the FBI, Gienapp said. "They were the ones that were going to catch that wrath" that Nichol felt for Nixon, he observed, not mentioning any of the other reasons Nichol might have been angry with the agency and the prosecution.

David Price said much the same: "It was a very strange time. Judge Nichol from Sioux Falls was tremendously angry at President Nixon. And . . .

I couldn't figure out what the FBI, which is supposed to find out facts, had to do with President Nixon, and what that had to do with the trial and why he was angry at the FBI. But that is the way he ruled. A judge is like God. And you do whatever he says. And his rulings were strange."

Along with Janklow, Price had unsuccessfully sued author Peter Matthiessen for assertions in his book *In the Spirit of Crazy Horse*. The lawsuit held up publication of the paperback version for eight years, but the court ultimately ruled in Matthiessen's favor. In the book Price emerges as AIM's greatest nemesis and bogeyman; AIM members interviewed by the author portrayed him as a right-wing operative out to destroy the movement. Matthiessen's style of reporting was to jot down anything an AIM member said to him and present it to readers as a verified fact, so it is hard to know how accurate this portrait is.

A journalist interrupted Price: Was it really so mind-boggling that a judge in the Democrats' camp would be so angry at J. Edgar Hoover's FBI?

"You're there to find facts," Price answered. "You're not there to take sides against AIM, the Wilson group, or anyone else. And present facts in court. That's it. You're not a political organization. Hoover was dead."

"For less than a year—"

"And he had produced an outfit that was clean and noncorrupt," Price responded. "And hardworking and did this country a service. And we did the civil rights investigations. . . . I don't even know what your question means."

As Gienapp and Price pursued their assertion that the government had lost its case because Nichol hated Nixon, Tilsen's preconference concerns were realized. Either the audience was not well acquainted with the Leadership Trial or it was more interested in other cases. Gienapp and Price's premise went unchallenged. An eight-month trial with 150 witnesses had been boiled down to a sound bite: "We lost because the judge hated Nixon." All of Nichol's reasons for being angry with the FBI and the prosecution went unmentioned. The fact that Nichol attempted to allow the jury's deliberations to continue after one member fell ill was never brought up.

Standing in the back of the room and wearing sunglasses was Ward Churchill, who now hammered Price about his involvement in the Aquash case. Like Russell Means, Churchill was a tall man. He had a deep voice that would have been well suited for radio, but, unlike Means, he never raised it or expressed anger when he offered his opinions and questions. A professor of ethnic studies, he had famously become a right-wing

punching bag in 2005 when his four-year-old es-
say about the 9/11 attacks received widespread
attention, particularly on Fox News. Through its
foreign policies, the United States had brought
the attacks on itself, Churchill had written. He
wasn't the first and only person to express this
point of view. But after the public spotlight was
turned on him, accusations of academic fraud
piled up—not coincidentally, he would say. Two
prominent Native American journalists refuted
his claims that he was of Indian descent. Churchill
said he was part Creek-Cherokee, but those na-
tions would only say that he did not possess the
blood quantum to be an enrolled member. His
story about being part of dangerous long-range
recon teams in Vietnam also didn't check out—
he had been trained as a truck driver.

The University of Colorado–Boulder fired
him for academic misconduct, which kicked off
a years-long legal battle that had continued to
that day. A lower court ruled that he had been
wrongfully terminated but awarded him dam-
ages of only one dollar. At the time of the conference, he was still appealing.

Whether or not Ward Churchill truly had
any Indian blood in him was beside the point.
There was no mistaking his passion for the cause.
An ardent and unrepentant left-wing academic,

he had lectured and written about the mistreatment of Native Americans since the 1970s. He had not been a member of AIM in its heyday, or in the dark years that followed the occupation, but he was well known as one of Means's closest confidants. Churchill pursued AIM's sorrowful "the-FBI-made-us-do-it" line of reasoning. The FBI had questioned and released Aquash twice, he said. He accused Price and the FBI of deliberately doing this in order to make her look like an informant. Indeed, putting a "snitch jacket" on a member of a left-wing or a white hate group was a well-known FBI tactic to create chaos and distrust among Hoover's targets in the 1960s.

"She was not an informant," Price insisted.

"I'm saying she was made to look like an informant," Churchill said.

It was a sad defense for the AIM members who had marched a bound woman to the side of a cliff, shot her in the back of the head, pushed her over, and let her body rot there. Price and Gienapp countered that it was not unusual for suspects to be released on bond, particularly women.

Kevin McKiernan brought up the charges that the FBI had used questionable testimony by Myrtle Poor Bear to help extradite Leonard

Peltier from Canada for the deaths of FBI agents Coler and Williams.

Price launched into a long, rambling answer of how Poor Bear's testimony came to be, and the circumstances that led the two agents to Oglala that fateful day; but eventually he abandoned his narrative in the interest of time. "You know, I can't do this," he said. "This is a three-hour story to tell you how the agents were killed and you can't go though it all." It was one of the few times the "incident at Oglala" was brought up during the conference, and the discussion went nowhere.

Among these back-and-forth disputes over points that had been argued for years, Adrienne Fritze emerged as a voice of reason. Perhaps, she said, it was time to put all this behind and move forward. Like Robinson's widow, Cheryl Buswell, she wanted some kind of forum where the participants could come clean, some kind of "truth telling and truth letting, where everybody's truth is allowed to be heard without opposition. . . . I would love for the rest of the conference to be committed to that outcome. Hold people to account, but hold them with love and understanding. Apologize if you need to. I certainly need to hear some apologies. We have that opportunity right here, right now."

The younger generation in the audience chimed in, lending their support to this suggestion. The first was Karin Eagle, a reporter for the *Native Sun News*, a Rapid City Native American newspaper that covered Pine Ridge. She was born after the occupation but raised during its aftermath. She directed her question to Price: "The rest of us, my generation, had to face being either good little Indians or radical bad Indians. And those terms were put on us by our relatives. If we went to school and did well in school and tried to better ourselves, we were 'the good sell-out Indians.' And if we stood up for our rights and spoke up for ourselves, people like you put us down. . . . That mentality—that you spoke with this morning in addressing this whole tragedy—that mentality has been kept alive for us forty years later. We're still dealing with that. . . . But I don't care anymore if I'm labeled a bad, radical Indian. I'm going to speak up. So that's what I'm going to do. . . .

"Do you think you contributed to the unrest even now on the reservation, so that we have to fight the battle still? You're not there. That root canal is still hurting us. We're still feeling it. Do you take any responsibility at all?"

Price replied: "I really appreciated my ignorance of the dynamics among Indian families and everything else. But I was never there as anything except an investigator. And in many ways, AIM needed something to hate. It needed something for headlines. . . . I was transferred. And I couldn't even smile at someone without the chance that they would be thought of as an informant. . . . I was there four years, not like you for a lifetime. I left, and I have never been back. My knowledge, you would all say, is that thin. . . . You can't fight with me over something I didn't do. . . . And part of the problem is, I don't know what the problem is. You live there, I don't. Now I'm babbling. I've been gone since 1977."

A young man who said he was an Iraq war veteran described growing up in the northeast corner of the reservation, near the town of Wanblee. As a boy he had to declare himself AIM or a Goon. AIM came to the reservation to save the Oglala Lakotas, he said. "You know what? They didn't need to come to Pine Ridge and try to save us that way. There is another side to it.

"I'm sorry that those agents were killed, because they had families too—just like a lot of the Indians that were killed. . . . I had to come here to say this. It is really sad how our two cultures are living like this to this day. If anything, maybe you folks might think about coming to the reservation and finding a way to heal. Because we live in a circle and our lives are a circle. And it was really sad to have to grow up living that way in Wanblee.

"No one has come back to the reservation and asked . . . to bring about a healing. There have been books written. Some have become movie actors. But no one has said, 'I'm going to come back to Wanblee. I'm going to come back to Porcupine, or Oglala, and I'm going to apologize to the whole community. And I want us to heal together.' No one has done that.

"And the Wounded Knee occupation—to me that is really a sacred place. That occupation should have been held somewhere else."

Price said he would not participate in any healing ceremonies.

"I wish you blessings. And I wish you well. But I don't want to be near it. It would be a disaster for me. I just wish you all well."

AFTERMATH

Hurd told the press that an eight-month trial which kept Banks and Means under wraps and not out fighting for their cause could serve as a deterrent to others. Indeed, any activist group that uses violence to achieve its goals in the United States will find itself spending more time in court and in prisons than on the streets. Such was the case for AIM. Banks spent most of the 1970s either on the lam or fighting extradition to South Dakota after being convicted of crimes stemming from the Custer courthouse riot. Both he and Means served time in South Dakota prisons for that incident. After Wounded Knee, neither attempted anything as audacious as an armed occupation again.

More than 150 trials stemmed from aspects of the occupation, with only about ten convictions. The Banks-Means leadership trial was supposed to set the tone, and it did. Despite the fact that it was something of a fiasco, the Justice Department pressed on with its attempts to convict dozens of rank-and-file AIM members, winning only light sentences against Holder, Camp, and Crow Dog from a no-nonsense judge in Iowa.

Meanwhile the Pine Ridge Reservation deteriorated precipitously. Not long after the occupation,

Carter Camp shot Clyde Bellecourt in the stomach. Pedro Bissonette was killed by BIA police. Coler and Williams were slaughtered by Banks's bodyguard Peltier, or someone standing within spitting distance of him. Anna Mae Aquash was shot execution style. By then the leadership schisms were manifest. The Bellecourts retreated to Minneapolis, where they continued their non-violent activism.

Dozens of attacks and many murders on Pine Ridge remain unsolved. A few months after the conference in August 2012, the U.S. attorney for South Dakota acquiesced to the Oglala Sioux Tribe's request to reopen many of these cases. Among the names on the list of fifty-six were Buddy Lamont, Frank Clearwater, and Pedro Bissonette. To this day former Goons accuse AIM members of committing these crimes, and vice versa. Through most of the 1980s AIM and Peltier enjoyed being a liberal cause célèbre—at least outside of South Dakota. *In the Sprit of Crazy Horse*, Peter Matthiessen's sloppily reported nonfiction book, became a best-seller despite—or because of—the Janklow and Price lawsuit. A *60 Minutes* piece exposed more FBI wrongdoing in the Peltier trial. AIM leaders cashed in on their notoriety, becoming speakers and professional activists, and in the case of Means a part-time

Aftermath

A chimney is the only structure remaining of the collection of residences and businesses that were destroyed in the final hours of the Wounded Knee occupation in 1973.

Hollywood actor, most notably in the 1992 hit movie *The Last of the Mohicans*. Meanwhile Pine Ridge retained its status as one of the poorest places in America.

Through the years, Joe Trimbach's hatred of AIM leaders appeared to fester. Historian Rolland Dewing would write: "FBI insiders say Trimbach's conduct at Wounded Knee plus his substandard performance at the ensuing trial at St. Paul blighted his chance of advancement. He was transferred to Memphis, Tennessee, in 1975 and retired in 1979." The Trimbachs' book, *American Indian Mafia*, targets not only AIM but anyone who has dared to question the FBI's behavior. Trimbach rails against his FBI superiors in Washington, the marshals, the army advisers at Wounded Knee, the media, PBS, authors Matthiessen and Hendricks, and especially Judge Nichol.

As the fortieth anniversary of the occupation approached, the spats over who were the good guys and who were the bad guys during the seventy-one-day siege and its aftermath promised to grow louder and more shrill.

PARTING BLOWS

The second-floor room of Morrison Commons, Augustana's student center with restaurants and bookstores, was a charmless spot to hold a luncheon, but the beef stew was good. It was the final meeting of the conference, and former Senator James Abourezk was the keynote speaker. As the attendees and honored guests ate, Means walked up to Dennis Banks and shook his hand, and the men exchanged a few words. During Means' bout with cancer the previous year, Banks had traveled to see his one-time friend and the two had put their differences behind them. It was Means who had alerted Banks about the conference and its often anti-AIM tone. So the movement's co-founder had packed up a couple of cars and taken off across the eastern edge of the prairie with many of his children and grandchildren in order to add his voice to the debate. The luncheon had been sold out, so the organizers had to scramble to find another table for Banks and his large retinue.

Once the spoons had been put down, Abourezk stood up behind the podium to speak. He began by saying that he felt "like Elizabeth Taylor's eighth husband. I know what's expected of me, but I'm not sure I can make it interesting."

Then he told in some detail the story of how he and McGovern went to Wounded Knee.

According to Abourezk, when the two senators made it inside he told Means, "Okay, we're here. Where are the hostages?" When they appeared, he said, "We have come to rescue you. We're here. You're safe. You can go now." But they said, "We're not going anywhere, we live here." That elicited chuckles from some members of the audience; but Adrienne Fritze, sitting at a table halfway across the room, was not laughing. "I had a hint there was some part of show business going on there," Abourezk continued.

He repeated his allegation that he had a deal to end the occupation, but Nixon administration officials conspired to keep it going so that the embattled president could look tough fighting the left-wing Indians.

"And I believe that's why they kept it going. I have no other—I'm just guessing—I have no other reason why they would not end it at the time," he said.

"Yesterday I had a little confrontation with Mr. Trimbach, who lied about my son's involvement in Anna Mae Aquash's death. He was nowhere near the place, and I don't mind calling Trimbach a liar twenty times if need be to tell him that. My son had nothing to do with that.

He was nowhere near there," Abourezk repeated, and accused the prosecutors of putting Looking Cloud on the stand at the Graham trial for "political reasons."

Bellecourt spoke next. He made an impassioned speech about the U.S government's attempt to wipe out traditional Indian culture throughout the twentieth century. "That's why we went to Wounded Knee. The organized religions, school, and BIA—they worked day in and day out to strip us of our land, our resources, our traditional way of life," he said. The rise of Indian casinos and the empowerment of the tribes that benefited from them, the American Indian Religious Freedom Act of 1978—all were the results of AIM's efforts, he asserted.

Banks, the shortest of the leaders, wore a black hat and a grey suitcoat over a bright red T-shirt. He wasted no time launching his counterpunches. He was familiar with Augustana College. In the summer of 1970 he had joined a conference there that was trying to persuade the Lutheran Church to do more about helping Native Americans. The call for action wasn't going as planned, so Banks and other non-AIM members occupied the dorm where they were being housed for a few days. The protest ended peacefully.

AIM co-founder Dennis Banks

"When I heard of the lineup of people who were going to be here," Banks said, "I felt that Augustana should be ashamed—should be ashamed of trying to arrange a confrontation, or trying to make people come together to be friends. I cannot be friends with people who have lied! People that have killed people! Add my name to the list of the people who want to call those people liars."

He recalled the morning he woke up in Wounded Knee only to find the valley surrounded by armored personnel carriers. "And inside the carriers, FBI agents, U.S. marshals, Goons, everybody that they could stick in there that was afraid to fight the .22s. That was afraid to fight the shotguns. And one AK-47. Against a force of three hundred people. . . .

"The vengeance that the FBI carries with them is that they lost the field of battle. They lost the field of battle in the courtroom. They lost the field of battle in the field itself. They were afraid. They were afraid of the American Indian Movement, a ragtag movement. . . . Their job was to destroy the American Indian Movement. But they didn't destroy us. Instead, they went on some sort of publishing campaign," Banks said, referring to the Trimbachs' book. While Banks had begun his comments by saying the college should be ashamed, he concluded by thanking the organizers.

Now it was time for questions. A journalist stood up from his table in the back and directed his question to Banks. "Can you tell us about your memory of the black civil rights activist Ray Robinson who came in the waning days of the occupation? What are your memories about him, and do you know anything about his fate?"

"Actually," said Banks, "I don't have any memories of him, because, I didn't know . . . I never met him. At least I don't recall meeting him. There were many people who came there. Over two thousand people during that time. . . ."

At that Means stood up from his table and took the microphone—though he didn't need it. He spoke loud enough for all to hear: "You know . . . it never stops here in South Dakota. Gienapp and R.D. Hurd were made judges, state judges in this state after the illegalities they participated in and led during our trial before and after. That being said, there is also the fact about Ray Robinson. I left allegedly to go negotiate with the White House after I was submitted to arrest. At any rate, I wasn't there when Ray Robinson allegedly showed up. But I do know this: I never heard of Ray Robinson until after 2002."

"Kevin McKiernan right here saw him," the journalist interjected, pointing to McKiernan who was sitting near the podium.

"I'm not talking about that," Means said. "I'm not arguing with you. I'm answering you. All right, and I'm telling you what I know. And I'm going to tell you this. No charges. From 1974 until 2002 did anyone ever hear of Ray Robinson. Did anyone ever shoot him or stab him or beat him or disappear him? It's a generation later that the bad-mouthing of Wounded Knee continues. You and people like you perpetuate this erroneous image you have of who we are. And I'm sick and tired of you bringing up these false accusations. Based on what? NOTHING!"

"I didn't accuse you of anything . . . "

"You *are* accusing. Don't give me that crap. Just bringing it up you're accusing. And you're writing about it. I don't want to hear about Ray Robinson anymore because it is a complete, absolute fabrication. MADE A GENERATION LATER! You didn't hear about it in the nineties, the eighties, or the seventies, or at our trial when all the illegalities were going on. They would have brought that up.

"And you people who want to continue to put AIM in this certain pocket of illegality—I can't stand you people, you know? And I wish I was a little bit healthier and a little bit younger. And I wouldn't just talk. I'm sick and tired. I've got children and grandchildren and great grandchildren, and you continue to besmirch the American Indian Movement that I love, the AIM that is responsible for this conference. We were the first constitutionalists. And that's what's wrong with this country. No one cares about the Constitution. Write about *that*, for crying out loud."

Some in the audience gave Means a round of applause. "J. Edgar Hoover is alive and well!" Bellecourt said, pointing at the journalist.

Once the harangue was over, Adrienne Fritze stood. She spoke in an even, measured voice that veiled her nerves. "Senator Abourezk, I remember you. I was a twelve-year-old hostage that they took at Wounded Knee. I have to say, I resent your comment about my family using or even thinking of using the media for their own purposes."

Abourezk seemed confused, and denied saying that his comments had referred to her family. He seemed taken aback that an audience member who was an eyewitness to his story had come forward.

"Then I apologize for mishearing what you said. I do remember you, and I do remember George McGovern, and I do recognize how frightening it was for you folks to be there."

Abourezk asked Fritze her name and how she was related to those in the village. She answered and suggested that AIM and its supporters had successfully whitewashed from history the fact that most of the Wounded Knee residents were of Native American heritage. "We didn't want to leave our homes. We didn't want to have our homes invaded. We did not want guns and knives pointed at us. We did not want our rights taken away. We had no voice, and we were under duress every moment we were there," she said.

She asked Means if he remembered the day she ran out of the house in hysterics when she saw a man riding her beloved horse. Means, looking away from her, avoiding eye contact, quietly said, "I do."

"[A guard] abused me and separated me from the rest of the group," Fritze said. "He was there to protect us. None of you knew, I don't think, that that occurred. There were other crimes that were committed against my family and several others."

A crater on Pine Ridge was left by the government, the FBI, and AIM—"a crater that hasn't been filled," she said. "Now, I'm not interested in retribution or revenge. I am sincerely interested in what this conference says it is interested in, which is reconciliation. I saw families torn apart by what was happening, when all we wanted as children was resolution. *We just want a resolution*. And we really didn't get it."

Both Means and Abourezk had been offered a chance to turn the page, but both refused. Abourezk retreated to his Nixon-administration conspiracy theory: "Do you believe me when I said that we could have ended it . . . and had a one-day siege? It could have ended that night, but the [Nixon administration] did not want—"

"I'm going to tell you the truth," Fritze interjected. "I don't believe any adult that was involved in anything at that time."

"Well, I'm sorry, but that's the truth," Abourezk said.

"No, I got it," Fritze said, exasperated. "I can't even say . . . I don't have anything in front of me as an adult woman to make a judgment about that."

Means also had his opportunity to deliver an apology, which at first he did. "I remember your trauma as a twelve-year-old," he said. "And I thank you for that contribution. And I'm really sorry for that trauma. But the people who you name were being traumatized by your family. There was the trader system that was prevalent on the Pine Ridge and the Navajo Indian reservation. And the traders held in economic bondage the people of Wounded Knee. Everyone forgets that. It was illegal for the commodity food program to go to anyone except Indian people. When we took over Wounded Knee, in every closet and under the beds was commodity food—illegally held by your family and your workers."

"Did you hear me say that we were tribal members?" asked Fritze.

Means went on, treating Fritze as if she were a hostile reporter, interrupting her several times as he went on a tirade against the corrupt trader system, and her family in particular, whom he accused of intercepting government-issued checks at the post office and taking money the Indians believed was owed to them. The same accusation had been made in several books. (Czywcznski, in one of the AIM trials, when questioned about his business practices, ninety-five times invoked the Fifth Amendment right not to incriminate himself.)

"Our takeover of Wounded Knee stopped that kind of abuse. The trader system died on Pine Ridge immediately after that. . . . I wanted you to know that. You were twelve years old, you couldn't realize the illegalities that were going on in that trader system."

Fritze again tried to speak in defense of her family, but Means talked over her. "I just want to make you aware that your older family members were not complete innocents," he concluded. As he often did, Means once again managed to get in the last word.

Finally, as Abourezk posed for pictures with Banks, Bellecourt, and Means, the attendees gave the speakers a round of applause.

For many, especially Adrienne Fritze, it had been an emotional and exhausting two days. She would go home empty-handed. Means's apology proved to be not much of an apology at all. The younger generation's calls for reconciliation over the two-day conference had been drowned out by the elders, who showed no signs of ending their battles of the 1970s.

As it turned out, the conference was Russell Means's last stand. He would not live to celebrate the fortieth anniversary of the Wounded Knee occupation. Five months later his cancer had returned. He died October 22, 2012, at his home in Porcupine, South Dakota.

NOTES, ACKNOWLEDGMENTS, SOURCES

More than a century after the Hotchkiss guns ceased firing over the Wounded Knee Valley in 1890, the debate over that horrific day continues. Who fired the first shot? Was it a battle or a massacre? The Lakotas have long memories. The injustices of the past do not fade easily, and December 1890 is still fresh in the minds of the victims' descendants. Pine Ridge Reservation remains one of the poorest places in America, and some lay the blame on the troubles produced by the occupation in the 1970s. Of course, there are many more factors than that. But the occupation, the deaths of Anna Mae Aquash and FBI agents Coler and Williams, and the imprisonment of Leonard Peltier may well be debated a century from now.

I do not normally care for the word "I" in journalism, so I left it out. The "journalist" mentioned throughout this piece, however, was myself. I went to the conference at Augustana College as a speaker and a reporter. I knew quite a bit about the early history of AIM and the tumultuous years on Pine Ridge Reservation that followed from my research into the Yellow Thunder incident and the history of Pine Ridge and the Nebraska border towns. I tried my best to bone up on the Wounded Knee occupation in the weeks before the conference, but I knew little about the Leadership Trial, which ended up being a major topic. Had I done my homework, I would have had more pointed questions for Judge Gienapp and the Trimbachs.

I would like to thank first and foremost my wife Nioucha for allowing me to get away for a few days to attend the conference, and for her support during the writing of this book. Thank you to conference organizers Harry Thompson and Tim Hoheisel for inviting me. Cheers to friends, far and wide, too numerous to mention, who pre-ordered this book so I could hire professional designers. Last, but not least, my deepest gratitude to Now and Then Reader Editor and Publisher Ivan R. Dee, who put the manuscript through the wringer, and improved it greatly.

The most difficult part of writing this story was deciding what to leave out. It was certainly challenging to summarize a two-day conference, the history of the AIM, and the Wounded Knee occupation and its aftermath without turning this into a full-fledged book. Obviously there is a great deal more to all these stories.

It was also difficult to reconcile two competing interpretations of history. I consulted several books and materials that I have found to be largely reliable, written by nonparticipants:

Rolland Dewing, *Wounded Knee II* (Manhattan, Kans., Great Plains Network, 2000).

Justin Hammer, "Race and Perception: The 1973 American Indian Movement Protest in Custer, South Dakota," master's thesis, University of South Dakota, May 2011.

Steve Hendricks, *The Unquiet Grave: The FBI and the Struggle for the Soul of Indian Country* (New York, Thunder's Mouth Press, 2006).

David J. Langum, *William Kunstler: The Most Hated Lawyer in America* (New York, New York University Press, 1999).

Stew Magnuson, *The Death of Raymond Yellow Thunder: And Other True Stories from the Nebraska–Pine Ridge Border Towns* (Lubbock, Texas Tech University Press, 2008).

Akim D. Reinhardt, *Ruling Pine Ridge: Oglala Lakota Politics from the IRA to Wounded Knee* (Lubbock, Texas Tech University Press, 2007).

John William Sayer, *Ghost Dancing the Law: The Wounded Knee Trials* (Cambridge, Mass., Harvard University Press, 1997).

No book or source is perfect, but the information in autobiographical works must be read with particular caution. Among those which I consulted are:

James Abourezk, *Advise and Dissent: Memoirs of South Dakota and the U.S. Senate* (Chicago, Lawrence Hill Books, 1989).

Dennis Banks and Richard Erdoes, *Ojibwa Warrior: Dennis Banks and the Rise of the American Indian Movement* (Norman, University of Oklahoma Press, 2004).

Barbara Deming, *Prison Notes* (Boston, Beacon Press, 1966).

William M. Kunstler, *My Life as a Radical Lawyer* (New York, Birch Lane Press, 1994).

Mark Lane, *Citizen Lane: Defending Our Rights in the Courts, the Capitol, and the Streets* (Chicago, Lawrence Hill Books, 2012).

Peter Matthiessen, *In the Spirit of Crazy Horse: The Story of Leonard Peltier and the FBI's War on the American Indian Movement* (New York, Penguin Books, 1991).

Russell Means, *Where White Men Fear to Tread: The Autobiography of Russell Means* (New York, St. Martin's Press, 1995).

Joseph Trimbach and John M. Trimbach, *American Indian Mafia* (Parker, Colo., Outskirts Press, 2008).

Other sources include:

Memorandum Decision, U.S. District Court, District of South Dakota, Western Division, *U.S. vs. Dennis Banks, U.S. vs. Russell Means*, October 9, 1974.

Email correspondence with Harry Thompson, and Elizabeth Thrond, of the Center for Western Studies, Augustana College, who provided background on the 1970 occupation of Bergsaker Hall.

"Ken Tilsen: Justice for All," *Minneapolis Star-Tribune*, November 7, 2007. http://www.startri bune.com/local/11590226.html?clmob=y& c=n&refer=y. Retrieved September 10, 2012.

"Widow of Civil Rights Activist Ray Robinson Wants Him Home," Associated Press, April 27, 2012. http://www.huffingtonpost.com/2012/ 04/27/ray-robinson-missing-civil-rights -activist_n_1458484.html. Retrieved September 26, 2012.

"Wounded Knee Defense Attorney Ken Tilsen Feels Snubbed," Native News Network, April 26, 2012. http://www.nativenewsnetwork.com /wounded-knee-defense-attorney-ken-tilsen -feels-snubbed.html. Retrieved September 10, 2012.

Follow-up phone interviews were conducted with Adrienne Fritze, Jeanne Fritze, and Paul DeMain. In the Fritzes' case, these were the first interviews given to a reporter or historian. In the past thirty-nine years no one had bothered to seek them out and put their memories on record. Complete transcripts of their interviews will be donated to the Oglala Lakota College archives.

INDEX

Italic page numbers indicate illustrations.

Index

ABOUT THE AUTHOR

 A native of Omaha, Nebraska, Stew Magnuson is the author of *The Death of Raymond Yellow Thunder: And Other True Stories from the Nebraska-Pine Ridge Border Towns*, which was named the 2009 Nebraska Nonfiction Book of the Year and a finalist for the Center of Great Plains Studies' 2008 Great Plains Distinguished Book of the Year. He also wrote *The Song of Sarin*, a fictional account of the 1995 subway gas attacks in Tokyo, Japan. He is currently managing editor of *National Defense Magazine*. A former foreign correspondent, Magnuson has filed stories from throughout Asia for wire services and various publications. He lives with his wife and daughter in Arlington, Virginia.

Read his column, "A View from a Wasicu," in the *Native Sun News*, or online at:

www.stewmagnuson.blogspot.com

Email: stewmag@yahoo.com

Website: www.stewmagnuson.com

ABOUT NOW & THEN READER

Now & Then Reader publishes original short form nonfiction for Kindle Singles, Apple Quick Reads, Kobo Books Short Reads and Barnes and Noble Nook Books. It concentrates on writings that are historically based but also have relevance for present day events with a focus on American History and European History.

Look for these titles at www.nowandthenreader.com:

Vigilante Wars: Gang Democracy and the Collapse of Government in San Francisco's Gold Rush Years, by Cecelia Holland

Selections from The Oregon Trail: The American West as It Once Was, by Francis Parkman

In Search of the Next Kick: Jack Kerouac and the Making of the Beat Generation, by John Tytell

Bonnie Parker Writes a Poem: How a Couple of Bungling Sociopaths Became Bonnie and Clyde, by Steven Biel

John F. Kennedy's Women: The story of a Sexual Obsession, by Michael O'Brien

Dawning of the Counter-culture: The 1960s, by William L. O'Neill

Don't Kill the Umpire: How Baseball Escaped Its Violent Past, by Peter Morris